Sex Pos

MW00885095

Your Guide to the 50 Best Sex Positions for a sexy marriage!

Check Out My Other Books!

Thanks for downloading my book! I am a firm believer that in order to have a fulfilling family life-one must be properly prepared and understand the fundamentals of relationships, how to be a good parent, and live an exciting and adventurous sex life. As you can see, I have written a series of multiple books on marriage, sex, and parenting. If you are looking to learn more about how to improve your marriage, sex and dating life, family life, etc.-please check out my other books! Simply click on the links below or search the titles below to check them out.

Parenting:

Parenting 101: 20 strategies to follow to raise well-behaved children

Raising Your Kids: Time Management for Parents for Stress-Free Parenting

Sex (General):

Sex Positions: Your Guide to the 50 Best Sex Positions for a sexy marriage!

Tantra Sex: The Beginner's Guide to 25 Tantra Techniques

Tantric Massage: Your Guide to the Best 30 Tantric Massage Techniques

BDSM Positions: The Beginner's Guide to 30 BDSM Techniques

Sex: Spice Up Your Sex Life! How to be maintain an awesome sex life with your partner and live your wildest sexual fantasies!

Sex Games: 35 Naughty Sex Games to make your Sex Life Hot!

Sex For Women:

Sexting: Sexting Tips for Women: 100 tips to turn him on!

Sex Positions for Women: The Ultimate Guide to the 50 Best Techniques to Turn Your Man On!

Talk Dirty: How to talk to get your man aroused and in the mood for sex!

Sex: The Hottest Tips for Better Orgasms!

Sex for Men:

Sex Positions for Men: The Ultimate Guide to the 50 Best Techniques to Turn Her On!

Dirty Talk: Talking Dirty for Men: 200 Examples to Get Your Girl Aroused and in the Mood for Sex!

Sex: Make her beg for more and be the best she's ever been with in bed!

Marriage:

Marriage and Sex: Why sex matters to keep romance alive!

Marriage for Women: Your Guide to a Happy, Fulfilling, Intimate Marriage!

Marriage for Men: How to be a good husband and have a happy, fulfilling, intimate marriage!

Marriage 101: How to have a long-lasting, happy and intimate marriage!

Wedding Planning: The Ultimate Guide to Budgeting and Planning your Wedding!

Marriage Communication: Your Guide to constructive praise, criticism, and communication for a happy, long-lasting marriage!

Divorce: Ten Steps to Preventing a Divorce and Save Your Marriage

Dating:

Tinder Dating: Your Guide to Creating a Strong Tinder Profile, Getting a First Date, and Being Confident!

Contents

Introduction

I want to thank you and congratulate you for downloading the book, *"Sex Positions: Your Guide to the 50 Best Sex Positions for a sexy marriage!"*

This book contains proven steps and strategies on how to develop a more meaningful, satisfying, and lasting relationship with your spouse through sex.

Every couple goes through a honeymoon period where they just can't seem to take their hands off each other. But as other aspects of the relationship grow more important, couples begin to realize changes in their sexual appetites. When one of you suddenly wants to make love less than the other, this leads to bitterness and disillusionment.

A waning libido is a common problem among couples who have been sleeping with each other for years and years. Contrary to what most might think, it's not just because you no longer find your partner attractive. Often, it's because *you* no longer find *yourself* attractive. When you look into the mirror, cringe, and decide that even *you* wouldn't sleep with you, this destroys your self-esteem. And in order to feel aroused, you need to feel that you are desired and that you're worthy of being wanted. Through this book, you'll find tips on how to be sexy in the bedroom. You'll learn that feeling sexy and having great sex is not about defying the sands of time. It's about getting the years to work *for* you instead of *against* you.

Sex and stagnancy don't mix. Couples who make a continuous effort to re-explore each other's bodies and find new ways to please each other are bound to last longer than those who don't. In this book, you'll find 50 of the best sex positions ranging from positions that can give her multiple orgasms to positions that can make him feel like the ultimate alpha male between the sheets.

Thanks again for downloading this book, I hope you enjoy it!

Chapter 1

Sex and Successful Relationships

> ➢ **Sex connects you.**

And not just physically but mentally and emotionally as well. Most couples will agree that nothing can make you feel closer to your partner than when you're making love with him/her. The mere act of being naked together makes you vulnerable to each other. Thus, the act of lovemaking fosters feelings of trust and acceptance. When sex is a satisfactory experience, you both feel a sense of security in each other's arms. After sex, the feel-good hormone oxytocin is released into your bloodstream. This provides you both with a sense of calm and contentment, therefore enabling you to bond with each other.

> ➢ **Sex makes your relationship smoother.**

When couples who have been together for a long time start to neglect each other in the bedroom, this creates a strain on the relationship. The effects tend to manifest themselves gradually though insecurities, irritability, and impatience. Even your partner's tiny quirks become the subject of heated discussions. Before you know it, you are subconsciously doubting and resenting each other. The worst thing is you don't even know where all these negative emotions are coming from, only that you're feeling them.

On the other hand, couples who have sex regularly are more easygoing and tolerant of each other's flaws. They are better able to sail smoothly through the daily trials they encounter in their relationship. Sex is a great stress-reliever and coming home after a hard day's work and getting some O's immediately pushes your buttons to love mode instead of battle mode. Furthermore, getting more O's can help you get better Zzz's and a great night's sleep leads to a fight-free morning. Couples find that once they get into fixing their bedroom issues, other issues in their marriage just sort of work themselves out.

> ➢ **Sex enables you to communicate with each other.**

When you're married or dating each other exclusively, sex is a language of love which you don't get to share with anyone else apart from your partner. There are some messages that are best expressed through touch and when you have sex with your spouse/lover, you tell him/her: *"I love you."*, *"I need you."*, and *"I want to be with you."*

Some couples think that as the sands of time screws up their libido, it becomes a message that it's time to start lying low. On the contrary, sex in marriage or in any long-term relationship doesn't have an expiration date. In fact, being together for so long gives you more excuses to get between the sheets more often. Why? Because your partner is that one person in this world who understands your body like no one else can. He/she has seen, touched, and loved every bit of you. Your long-time lover knows what makes you tick. He/she knows what makes you go wild and soft, what makes you feel alive, and what makes you feel loved. Each time you make love, you remind each other why you belong with each other and why no one else will do.

> ➢ **Sex helps you to build each other up.**

When you have sex, you tell your partner how much you value him/her. The mere act of initiating sex reassures your partner that you still find him/her attractive after all these years. When you show interest in each other, you boost each other's egos. When you offer yourselves to each other and marvel in its each other's bodies, it sends these messages: *"I'm happy to be yours."* and *"I'm proud that you're mine."*

> ➢ **Having sex more often keeps thoughts of infidelities away.**

If you start neglecting your partner, this negatively affects his/her self-esteem. This makes your spouse/lover wonder about the causes of your waning affection. Once a seed of doubt has been planted, there's no stopping its evil branches from growing. Her/his speculations may range from *"He's having an affair."* to *"She doesn't love me anymore."*

Furthermore, such undesirable thoughts can push either one of you to seek happiness, comfort, and pleasure somewhere else. This can lead you to explore dangerous what ifs and what-might-have-beens (example: *"What if I'd married my ex instead, maybe I would've been happier."* or *"I don't think it's my fault. I think I still got it. Maybe I should try it with someone else."*)

> ➢ **Having sex regularly helps you to grow old together *gracefully*.**

When one of you is suffering from a physical illness, the relationship also suffers. You'll spend too much time, thought, and energy into worrying about the medical bills and the future and when this happens, tenderness and affection takes a backseat. The fact is, when you're too preoccupied with your own pain, you don't have much care left in you to share with your partner. Moreover, couples with poor levels of health are prone to irritability and thus, making them vulnerable to domestic disputes.

A romp in the sheets is a fun and pleasurable way to burn calories. By turning sexy time into your cardio, you're helping each other stay physically fit. Regular sex reduces the risk of bone diseases (pun not intended), heart disease, and prostate cancer. Keep those hormones flowing to get the benefit of glowing skin and to tame those merciless menopausal symptoms. Sex is also a great immune system booster. Likewise, it enhances your capacity to deal with stress. Improve each other's health and prolong each other's lives so you can make more beautiful memories together.

Chapter 2

How to be Sexy in the Bedroom and How to Maintain a Great Sex Life

When you and your long-time lover have been at it for years, it has the following effects:

- less self-consciousness
- less mystery
- less spontaneity

> ➤ **Successful couples pay attention to pre-sex prepping.**

Your partner has seen it all so you shouldn't have to worry about shaving off your pubes, right? And since you love each other, it shouldn't matter if you skip the shower, right? Wrong! Being married for years and even being madly in love is no excuse for shortchanging your sexual soulmate. You need to perform pre-sex prepping as diligently as you did during the honeymoon phase of your relationship. Wear cologne like you used to. Invest in sexy lingerie like you used to. This will prevent your spouse from forgetting what attracted him/her to you in the first place. Furthermore, prepping your body for sex makes your partner feel special. It makes them feel that you still value what they think and that their desire is still worth earning.

The problem with some couples is that they find it awkward to talk to each other about sex and hygiene. To others, it's easier to just have sex less often than to risk embarrassing, provoking, or hurting their partner in a conversation about stubbles and body odors. So don't wait for your husband/wife to tell you that you need to take care of yourself because they probably won't. It's your job anyway and no one has to tell you to do these things. To put it bluntly: If you want more oral action, shave your nether regions.

That said, pre-sex prepping doesn't have to be a boring chore. In fact, you can even do it together. Start your foreplay in the shower by soaping each other's bodies.

> ➤ **Smart couples know that they have to look, think, feel, and be sexy.**

When you no longer find yourself attractive, this lowers your libido. Low self-esteem cripples your capacity to become open to new sexual adventures. A woman might be afraid of trying a new sex position because she's worried about how big her butt will look like. A man might feel threatened by prolonged foreplay because he might be unable to maintain his erection. In order to be sexy, you need to look, think, and feel the part. Preparing your body for sex shouldn't be done just prior to a lovemaking session. Instead, it should be something that you incorporate in your lifestyle. When you exercise, maintain a balanced diet, and rehydrate you are priming your body for lovemaking. A positive body image will make you more confident in bed. Provide yourself with positive affirmations (ex. "My body is beautiful.", "I am sexy within and without.")

Being physically fit will significantly improve your bedroom performance. Additionally, kegels exercises for women helps in toning the butt, the lower back, and the abdomen so she can effectively use these muscles to position herself during sex. Thus, allowing her to get more G-spot stimulation and more orgasms. Likewise, kegels exercises for men will help him in achieving ejaculatory control. Meanwhile, specific exercises like ball crunches can help improve his thrusting power.

> ### Clever couples understand that familiarity breeds boredom.

Sure, you've memorized every hair, every mole and explored every nook and cranny of each other's bodies but this is not an excuse to let the mystery jump out the window. Mystery equals to excitement and it's something that we all subconsciously crave. When this element disappears, that's when you start wondering and fantasizing about how it would feel like to have sex with other people. Not everyone will act on these fantasies but unfortunately, there are those who do.

To keep your spouse from straying, change things up in the bedroom. It doesn't have to be a drastic change. It can be as simple as a haircut or a new sex position that you haven't tried before. Readjust your carnal clock. That is, if you're used to making love in at night, rub up against your spouse early in the morning. Turn familiar objects and places into things and areas of mystery. Example: Make pantry staples even yummier by introducing food into foreplay. Surprise your spouse with an erotic buffet by placing fruits, whip cream, chocolate, and other edibles all over your body for him/her to feast on. Your partner will never see the kitchen in quite the same way.

> ### A passive lover is no lover at all.

So, are you a person or a blow-up doll? When you just lie there like you're bestowing your spouse a grand favor, you make your partner feel as though he/she is not worth your effort. This, in turn, kills their motivation, leading to mediocre performance. Furthermore, letting your partner do all the work implants in his/her brain that sex is nothing more than a routine activity. Remember that nothing can kill passion quicker than monotony. Motivate your partner by taking the lead from time to time. Sex should be a complete tactile, visual, and auditory experience. Even when your lover is on top, motivate him/her by sexy sounds and facial expressions. A woman can touch herself while her husband is making love to her. Likewise, a man can whisper words of affection (or talk dirty) while his wife is making love to him. Even when your partner is doing all the thrusting, do your part by stroking, kissing, and licking his/her erogenous spots. Moreover, eye contact deepens the intimacy of the act so even when you're all tied up, you can still participate by expressing your love (and lust) through your eyes.

➢ Wise couples don't just do it. They talk about it.

If there's anything that's more intimate than having sex, it's talking about sex. You become sexier to your partner if you can listen to his/her sexual suggestions with an open mind. Stay in tune with each other's erotic desires by openly discussing your fantasies and fetishes. Make a bucket list of the sex positions that you'd like to try, places that you'd like to have sex in, games and toys that you'd like to introduce in the boudoir, etc. Be sure to make this a fair give and take activity. When your partner feels that you're that one person in the world who can listen and make love to him/her without judgment and inhibitions, that's when you're at your sexiest.

Chapter 3

50 Best Sex Positions for Men and Women

Rear Entry Positions

Men love entering women from behind because this position feels very primal. Rear entry positions are also favorable for women who love a strong feeling of fullness during intercourse.

➤ **Traditional Doggie Style**

In this position, the woman gets down on her hands and knees with her legs somewhat apart. After this, the man positions himself on his knees and penetrates her from behind.

➤ **Turtle Style**

The woman kneels on the floor and then brings her body downwards. She does this so that her buttocks are lying on the back of her ankles. Next, she leans her body forward as far as it can go. The man then penetrates her from the rear.

➤ **Frog Style**

To do this, the woman should assume a squatting position. Then, she needs to lean forward. She should place her hands in front of her and make sure that they're flat on the floor. This will help her balance herself. Next, the man kneels behind her and enters her ala traditional doggie style.

➤ Basset Hound Style

The woman first positions herself on all fours. Next, she has to lower her body onto the floor, spreading her knees outward while pushing her buttocks up towards her partner. She then lowers herself to her elbows so that her chest is near the floor. Afterwards, the man penetrates her from behind.

➤ Corner Doggie Style

The woman assumes a standing position while placing one of her legs on either side of the bed corner. After this, she leans over toward the bed while supporting herself with her elbows. Next, the man enters her from the rear just as he would during the traditional doggie style.

➤ Rear Admiral Style

The couple starts off by standing while facing the same direction. Then, the man penetrates the woman from behind. After this, she bends over so that her abdomen is parallel to the ground. One of them should spread his/her legs open while the other keeps his/her own together. The couple can decide to take turns.

➤ Fire Hydrant Style

The first thing to do would be to have the woman position herself like she would in the traditional doggie style. Her partner should position himself behind her on his knees. He will then lift one of his legs, bring it forward, and place his foot on the ground to the woman's side. As he does this, he lifts her leg. This way, her thigh will be lying on top of his thigh.

➤ Bulldog Style

Compared to the classic doggie, the bulldog places the woman on a more submissive role. She gets down on her hands and her knees. Then the man and the woman have to bring their legs together. Afterwards, the man squats down a bit and then penetrates his partner from behind. His feet are situated outside of the woman's legs. Meanwhile, his hands are around her waist.

Deep Entry Positions that'll Make Husbands Go Crazy

Men love the feeling of going in deep into their partner. Apart from the exquisite physical pleasure that makes them want to ejaculate quickly, it provides them with a feeling of power and abandon.

> ➤ **Anvil Style**

In this position, the woman lies on her back. Meanwhile, she should keep her legs wide open. The man then lifts the woman's legs towards her chest. Afterwards, he moves over her, using his arms to support himself. Next, he asks her to rest her lower legs on either side of his head so they're touching his shoulders.

> ➤ **Drill Style**

The couple begins with the traditional missionary position, with the woman on her back and the man on top of her. Then, the woman spreads her legs. The man moves on top of the woman. As he does this, she draws up her legs and uses them to embrace her lover's waist.

> ➤ **Deep Impact Style**

Lying on her back, the woman points her legs skyward. Meanwhile, the man is to position himself on his knees facing her. Then, she rests her legs on each of her partner's shoulders. Next, he grabs her by the thighs and performs deep thrusts.

➢ Jockey Style

The couple begins by having the woman lie face down on the mattress. She's supposed to keep her legs together. Meanwhile, her lover straddles her, placing his knees on either side of her waist. This looks like he's riding a horse, hence the name. The jockey is perfect for either anal or vaginal penetration.

➢ Cello Player Style

This is done by having the woman lay on her back and then lift her legs in such a way that they're pointing upward. Meanwhile, the man should kneel upright while penetrating her. Next, the woman rests both her legs on *one* of her lover's shoulders. One of the man's arms is to be wrapped around the woman's lower leg. Meanwhile, his other arm should be wrapped around her thighs.

Dominant Male Positions

The following power positions are for men who like playing the role of the dom in the bedroom. These positions require the woman to be physically vulnerable and at his mercy, so to speak. He also gets total control of the pacing and the power of his thrusts. These are also perfect for women who like playing the role of the sub.

➢ Viennese Oyster Style

The woman lies down on her back and spreads her legs wide open. Grabbing her legs, she pulls them in towards herself until her knees are very close to the bed. Then, to make sure that her legs stay in place, she puts her arms at the back of her knees. The man then penetrates her.

➢ Down Stroke Style

The woman should be lying on the edge of the bed. She needs to raise her legs in the air so that they're pointing upward. Meanwhile, the man is to stand in front of the woman. He grabs the woman's legs and then pulls her body up towards his so he can enter her. Each time he thrusts downwards, he raises her body to meet his.

➢ Bridge Style

The woman should be on all fours. But here's the catch: Her back should be towards the ground and her body should be facing the ceiling. Facing his partner, the man kneels and positions himself between her legs. With his hands grabbing her thighs, he enters her while pulling her body close to his.

➢ Suspended 69

This is actually an exotic oral sex position that requires a great deal of power and flexibility. Be warned that this is a potentially dangerous position so it's not for everyone.

The man first lies down on his back. His feet, however, should be draped on the side of the bed, not so much as dangling, but with his feet played firmly on the floor. Next, his partner is to climb on top of him to position herself in a traditional 69. Keeping her legs together, she hugs her lover's head with them.

After a while, the man should try to sit up. Meanwhile, the woman is to make sure that her legs are still holding the back of her lover's neck. The next and the most crucial step would be to gauge whether it's still comfortable to perform oral sex on each other while maintaining this pose. Then, with the woman's arms embracing the man's waist, he gradually assumes a standing position.

Intimate Positions that Wives Love

Women particularly love sex positions that provide them not just with physical pleasure but also with a feeling of closeness with their partner.

➢ Spooning Style

The couple lies down on their sides while facing the same way. The man should be behind the woman. Then, he penetrates her from behind. The woman moves her top leg forward a bit to help the man enter her as he leans over. He then wraps her in his arms.

➢ Sporking Style

The couple starts by lying on their right side, with the man behind the woman. The woman then leans forward and takes her legs towards her upper torso.

➢ Side Entry Missionary Style

The woman needs to lie on her side while keeping her legs together and bending them a little. She may turn her body to face her partner who will have to be on top of her. He is to enter the woman from behind while he's positioned on his knees. So basically, it's like he's doing the missionary while his woman is in a side-lying position.

➢ Sofa Style

In this position, the man sits on the sofa with his feet flat on the floor. Facing him, the woman then squats on her partner and utilizes her legs to help her move up and down.

➢ Pearly Gates Style

Facing upward, the couple lies together. The man should bend his knees a little and make sure that his feet are planted on the mattress. The woman then lies on top of the man while still facing upward. So it's kind of like an upward version of spooning.

> ### Lotus Style

The man should be seated cross-legged, yoga style. Then, facing her partner, the woman lowers herself onto him. The man and the woman then wrap their arms around each other's bodies.

Positions to Give Women Multiple Orgasms

> ### Butterfly Style

While laying on her back, the woman's hips should be situated near the edge of the bed. The man stands at the foot of the bed and raises her hips, allowing her thighs to rest on his chest. The woman's lower legs should be resting on each of his shoulders.

> ### Criss Cross Style

Lying on her back, the woman raises her legs until they are pointing to the ceiling. Standing up straight, the man enters her. Making sure that the woman's legs are still straight, he crosses them at the ankles thus, creating a super tight fit.

> ### Fast Love Style

In this position, the man lies down with his knees slightly bent and his feet flat on the floor. The woman then straddles him while's she's on her feet. This is a nice quickie position for women who feel a sudden urge.

> ## Missionary Style

The woman lies on her back while keeping her legs open. Her partner positions himself on top of her in such a way that his legs are situated between hers. For support, the man may rest his elbows on either side of his partner.

Positions for Maximum G-spot Stimulation

> ## Bent Spoon Style

The man lies on his back and the woman lies on top of him, also on her back. This way, they're both looking up the ceiling. The man penetrates the woman. Meanwhile, she extends her arms outward. The man needs to keep his legs open. Then, the woman draws her knees up towards her upper body and allows her feet to rest on top of her lover's knees.

> ## Italian Hanger Style

The couples needs to first have sex in the classic missionary position. Then, somewhere during the middle, the man gets on his knees, bringing them close to his partner's body. As a result her legs will be spread wider apart. Then, he places his hands beneath her buttocks and raises her hips. He then proceeds with his thrusts.

Positions for Maximum Clitoral Stimulation

> ## Coital Alignment Technique

The woman lies on her back with her partner on top of her. How is this different from the missionary? He has to move his body forward over the woman's as opposed to thrusting in and out of her. This changes the angle of penetration so that his penis is able to stimulate her lower vaginal wall. This way, his pubic bone is in direct contact with her clitoris.

➢ **Thigh Tide Style**

Lying on his back, the man tries to keep his legs straight while spreading them to some degree. Then, he lifts one knee in such a way that his foot is planted firmly on the mattress. The woman straddles his raised knee and lowers herself onto her lover's penis with her back against him. Then, she performs up and down movements, which will allow her to rub her clitoris against her partner's thighs.

➢ **Sandwich Style**

The man penetrates the woman ala missionary style while's she's lying on her back with her legs spread open and pulled back towards her chest. He then places one hand under each of her knees to adjust the angle of penetration.

Woman-on-Top Positions for Fierce Females

Women enjoy these positions because it provides them with a sense of empowerment and allows them to control the pace of lovemaking thus, enabling them to achieve orgasms. Men also love woman-on-top positions because it enables them to relax and just open themselves up for pleasure. Additionally, it provides them with a sensational view of their partner's body.

➢ **Cowgirl Style**

The man lies down on his back while the woman assumes a kneeling position as she straddles him. Her legs are supposed to be situated on either side of her lover's waist. She then proceeds to bouncing up and down or grinding on top of him. By moving her body backward or forward, she is able to regulate the angle of penetration.

> ### ➤ Reverse Cowgirl Style

This is pretty much the same as the cowgirl style. The main difference is that the woman has her back to her partner as she straddles him and bounces or grinds on top of him.

> ### ➤ Asian Cowgirl Style

This is another variation of the cowgirl sex position. The major difference is that the woman squats with her feet on either side of her lover's body instead of being on her knees. Her feet will therefore be carrying her weight. Her hands may rest on her partner's chest or on either side of him.

> ### ➤ Bucking Bronco Style

While the man lies on his back, the woman faces him and then gets on top of him. She then guides his penis inside her. After he has penetrated her, she leans backwards while placing her arms behind her. After this, she places her feet on either side of her partner's head.

> ### ➤ Rodeo Style

This sex position is a variation of the reverse cowgirl. Facing towards her partner's feet, the woman straddles him while on her knees. The man's job here is to thrust really hard and fast, almost as if he's attempting to buck his partner off him. Meanwhile, she holds on tight and rides the rodeo!

> ### ➤ Amazon Style

In this dominant woman-on-top position, the woman asks her partner to lie on his back and tells him to draw his legs up and bend his knees. As he pulls his legs towards his upper torso, she squats down on him and carefully pulls his penis backwards to guide him inside her.

➤ **Crab Style**

While lying on his back, the man should keep his legs together. The woman then straddles him, placing her legs on either side of his body. After this, she leans backward with her hands and arms extended behind her. She makes love to him by moving her body up and down while using her arms for support. She may also choose to perform rotating maneuvers with her hips.

➤ **Missionary Style with Woman on Top**

This is different from the traditional missionary style because the woman will be taking the top position. The woman should first ask her partner to lie down with his legs straight. Then, she straddles him while on her knees. Next, she leans her body forward and rests her elbows on the bed.

Man-on-Top Positions for Women who Love Dominant Men

Women love having sex with men who are confident and know what they're doing in bed. By taking control, he is allowing her to just relax and focus on receiving pleasure.

➤ **Cowboy Style**

While on her back, the woman makes sure that she keeps her legs together as her partner straddles her. The man's legs are situated on either side of her body. Meanwhile his bum is resting right on top of his partner's legs.

> ➢ **Deckchair Style**

The couples start off in the missionary position. Then, the man gets into his knees while inserting his arms under the each of the woman's knees. His hands are placed on the bed for support. Meanwhile, the woman remains positioned on her back while raising her legs into the air. By assuming this position, they get to stimulate areas that don't get much attention when having sex in the traditional missionary position.

> ➢ **Launch Pad Style**

The woman lies on her back. Meanwhile, the man is on his knees facing her. He enters her and as he does this, she raises her legs skyward, drawing her knees towards her upper body. Then, she allows her feet to rest on her partner's chest.

> ➢ **Victory Style**

The man is on top while the woman lies on her back and spreads her legs open, holding it up in a V shape. The man then performs thrusting movements while on his knees.

> ➢ **Exposed Eagle Style**

It's best to begin this position with the classic cowgirl. Once there, the woman leans backward until her back is on top of her lover's knees and his thighs. Then, the man lifts the upper part of his body so that he's seated upright.

Quickie Positions

Nothing turns on a man or a woman more than knowing that his/her sex soulmate wants to have sex with him/her anytime, anywhere. As such, you must have an arsenal of quickie sex positions up your sleeve.

➢ Bodyguard Style

Couples start off by standing upright and facing the same way. The man should be positioned behind the woman. Then, with the back part of her body pressed against his front, he penetrates her from behind.

➢ Bendover Style

The couple first performs the bodyguard sex position. After he's inside her, she leans her body forward with her arms extended. She lowers her body until her hands are resting on the ground. Then, the man starts thrusting in and out of her.

➢ Burning Man Style

This sex position is best done on a countertop. The woman bends over so that her tummy is resting over the countertop. Meanwhile, her feet should be planted firmly on the floor. This will help keep her in place because this position is designed for hard and fast thrusting, hence the name. Her partner then proceeds to entering her from the rear. Couples can use this whether they want to make love vaginally or anally.

➢ Dancer Style

The couple stands facing each other. Then, the woman raises one of her legs and envelops her man's body with it. Next, the man penetrates her and begins thrusting. To make sure that his partner stays in place, the man may wrap his arms around her while supporting her raised leg with his hand.

➢ Pump Style

If you want to have sex by a wall, perform this position by having the woman assume a sitting position in the air. The woman's legs should be bent a little. The man stands beside her and penetrates her from the rear. He then proceeds to thrusting in and out while grabbing onto her waist. To keep herself steady, she may extend her arms and press them against the wall.

Conclusion

Thank you again for downloading this book!

I hope this book was able to help you to understand and appreciate the value of sex in keeping relationships alive.

The next step is to apply these bedroom tips and to try out these sex positions to help lovemaking become the exciting, fulfilling, and nurturing experience that it's supposed to be. May this be the beginning of a fun and intimate adventure between you and your significant other.

Finally, if you enjoyed this book, then I'd like to ask you for a favor, would you be kind enough to leave a review for this book on Amazon? It'd be greatly appreciated!

Thank you and good luck!

Sex Games:

35 Naughty Sex Games to make your Sex Life Hot!

Check Out My Other Books!

Thanks for downloading my book! I am a firm believer that in order to have a fulfilling family life-one must be properly prepared and understand the fundamentals of relationships, how to be a good parent, and live an exciting and adventurous sex life. As you can see, I have written a series of multiple books on marriage, sex, and parenting. If you are looking to learn more about how to improve your marriage, sex and dating life, family life, etc.-please check out my other books! Simply click on the links below or search the titles below to check them out.

Parenting:

Parenting 101: 20 strategies to follow to raise well-behaved children

Raising Your Kids: Time Management for Parents for Stress-Free Parenting

Sex (General):

Sex Positions: Your Guide to the 50 Best Sex Positions for a sexy marriage!

Tantra Sex: The Beginner's Guide to 25 Tantra Techniques

Tantric Massage: Your Guide to the Best 30 Tantric Massage Techniques

BDSM Positions: The Beginner's Guide to 30 BDSM Techniques

Sex: Spice Up Your Sex Life! How to be maintain an awesome sex life with your partner and live your wildest sexual fantasies!

Sex Games: 35 Naughty Sex Games to make your Sex Life Hot!

Sex For Women:

Sexting: Sexting Tips for Women: 100 tips to turn him on!

Sex Positions for Women: The Ultimate Guide to the 50 Best Techniques to Turn Your Man On!

Talk Dirty: How to talk to get your man aroused and in the mood for sex!

Sex: The Hottest Tips for Better Orgasms!

Sex for Men:

Sex Positions for Men: The Ultimate Guide to the 50 Best Techniques to Turn Her On!

Dirty Talk: Talking Dirty for Men: 200 Examples to Get Your Girl Aroused and in the Mood for Sex!

Sex: Make her beg for more and be the best she's ever been with in bed!

Marriage:

Marriage and Sex: Why sex matters to keep romance alive!

Marriage for Women: Your Guide to a Happy, Fulfilling, Intimate Marriage!

Marriage for Men: How to be a good husband and have a happy, fulfilling, intimate marriage!

Marriage 101: How to have a long-lasting, happy and intimate marriage!

Wedding Planning: The Ultimate Guide to Budgeting and Planning your Wedding!

Marriage Communication: Your Guide to constructive praise, criticism, and communication for a happy, long-lasting marriage!

Divorce: Ten Steps to Preventing a Divorce and Save Your Marriage

Dating:

Tinder Dating: Your Guide to Creating a Strong Tinder Profile, Getting a First Date, and Being Confident!

Introduction

Are you looking to bring your sex up a notch? Do you have a more naughty, kinky side to you?

Then this book is for you! Throughout this book you will learn naughty oral sex tips, rough sex tips, and some sex games all to spice up your sex life! Sex is exciting and should always be exciting. This book shows you how to always do that.

Here is a synopsis of what you will learn:

-What Naughty Sex Is

-Naughty Oral Sex Tips for Him

-Naughty Oral Sex Tips for Her

-Rough Sex Tips

-35 Sex Games

Chapter 1 – Naughty Sex Basic Tips

Don't get caught up in vanilla sex! You are on a quest for a more exciting, sexy, and kinky sex life. Don't apologize for wanting to make things a little more naughty in your relationship. Here are some basics ideas to make your sex life more naughty:

Being submissive:

Both men and women fantasize about this. It is dead sexy to have your partner completely in control and completely have their way with you!

Being dominant:

This is the complete opposite of being submissive. You know you love the idea of tying your partner down and doing whatever you want with them!

Group sex:

Everyone fantasizes about this. Men love to fantasize about a threesome with their wife/girlfriend along with a hot Asian or Latina woman involved. There's nothing sexier than having anal sex with your wife/girlfriend while watching her eat out another woman's pussy!

Women typically fantasized being worshipped by her partner and another man. One man can penetrate her while the other receives a blowjob from her.

A great way to make this fantasy a reality is to join a local swinger club. Couples are encouraged to live out their fantasies there!

Exhibitionism:

Some sort of public sex-whether it be filming a porno between you and your partner-or fucking in a public place are fantasies all men and women are likely to have at some point in their lives.

Filming a porno is not recommended for obvious reasons. While it is legal it can have serious professional consequences if your friends/families/coworkers find out! Having sex in a public area is a much more commonly fulfilled fantasy. However-use with caution and make sure you don't get caught, as this can have serious legal consequences!

Strap on sex:

This is a fantasy held by women where they play the "man" for the night and wear a "strap-on" penis. Both the woman and even the man have fun with this-as the woman will enjoy being the aggressor for the night and penetrating the man. Having her man vulnerable to this kind of sex is an incredible turn-on for women. You can purchase a strap-on penis at a local adult store.

Juicy Sex:

Both sexes fantasize about their partner releasing all their juices all over their faces/bodies. Have sex to the point where either the woman squirts all over the man or the man cums all over the woman's body.

Chapter 2 – Naughty Oral Sex Tips for Her:

If you are a man reading this book-have your wife or girlfriend read this section. This chapter reveals some naughty tips for her to devour you down there!

Invisible Oral:

Turn the lights out while you devour his cock. This element of surprise is exciting to him because he doesn't know what you will do to him. The lack of sight also enhances his sensations down there.

Gagging:

Take his cock and suck on it. Bring it as far into your throat as you can so that you are not choking on it but just enough to make you gag. This will drive him crazy.

Ambush him at the door:

A quick unexpected blowjob when he least expects it when he walks through the door at home is sexy. About 34% of men wish that their woman would surprise them with oral sex as they walk through the door. When he walks through the door, kiss him, ask him how his day was, and then surprise him by ripping his cock out and giving him head.

Spit on it!

A sexy thing to do before you give your man a blowjob is to spit on his cock. Massage his cock and rub the saliva all over the shaft and head of his penis. This makes his cock stickier and juicier. You can also do this to his balls, perineum and butthole as well.

Play with his balls and pressure his perineum:

Don't neglect the balls. Playing with his balls is a must when it comes to oral, because they are often neglected during intercourse. Cradle his balls, suck each one in your mouth, nibble a little, and don't forget to stroke. While you are caressing the balls, go towards the shaft and go up and down with your tongue.

The perineum (the area between his penis/balls and his butt) is also often ignored too. This is an extremely sensitive area for both men and women. Nibble this area, kiss it up and down, and put pressure with your finger down there.

Lick the tip of his cock:

The meatus-which is the hole that is the tip of his penis-is an extremely sensitive area. Licking and applying pressure with your tongue there is a huge turn on.

Be enthusiastic and horny:

Many guys are worried that their wife/girlfriend do not like giving head. Show him you love it! Suck his cock aggressively and smile while you do it. Bonus if you can make seductive eye contact with him while you are at it.

The Breast Stroke:

Lie on your back and have your man place his penis between your boobs. Have him thrust towards your face. Tilt your head towards your boobs and open your mouth and catch his cock inside your mouth every time he makes a thrust.

Attack multiple areas:

If you want your man to cum more easily, make sure your mouth and hands are both always busy. When you are sucking on his penis, play with his balls and massage his perineum. When you are licking and kissing his butt, massage his cock and his balls. Double or triple the sensation for him and he will cum all over the place.

A Hot Spot:

A hot spot women often miss is a patch of skin on his penis that is right between his cock's base and testicles. Gently nibbling and sucking on that area will make him lose his mind.

Rim Jobs:

If you don't know what a rim job is-it is the art of sucking, licking, and kissing your partner's butthole. Rim jobs, if done right, can be seriously hot. Make sure your man has showered previously (for obvious reasons.....). Have your man take the "face down, ass up," position. Lick and suck the back of his cock, and then slowly lick the shaft of his cock upwards toward his balls. Continue to massage his cock while you now kiss and lick his balls. Gently nibble on both of his balls while moving upward to his perineum. Gently nibble and lick on his perineum while you continue to massage his cock and balls. Finally, kiss the area around his butthole, and then devour his butthole with your tongue. You can also spit on his butthole and rub the saliva from his butthole down to his balls and cock. This will all surely drive him crazy.

Chapter 3 – Naughty Oral Sex Tips for Him:

If you are a woman reading this book-have your husband or boyfriend read this section. This chapter reveals some naughty tips for her to devour you down there!

Use your hands:

Grab her buttcheeks while you are driving your tongue into her pussylips. This intensifies the feeling. Giving oral without using your hands properly is just awkward. You can also finger fuck her from the bottom of her pussy while licking her at the same time.

For maximum orgasm it is important to always use your hands. When you are eating her pussy, make sure you are either fingering her or squeezing her buttcheeks. When you are licking and kissing her butt, continue to massage or finger her pussy.

Spit on it!

A sexy thing to do before you give your woman oral is to spit on her pussy. Massage her pussy and rub the saliva all over the lips of her vagina. This makes her pussy juicier. You can also do this to her perineum and butthole as well.

Switch between aggressive and passive oral sex:

Start out slow. Gradually kiss her inner thighs, her perineum, and gently rub her clitoris with one finger. Then slowly move towards kissing her pussylips. Afterwards, slowly enter 1 finger into her pussy. Then move to two fingers or more. The key though is to move slowly.

Afterwards, aggressively give her pussy or butt a tongue attack. Women love a man who can consistently switch between slowly and deeply giving her love and aggressively giving her love.

Food Sex:

Why eat your dinner off of platters and silverware when you can eat off of each other's naked bodies? Give this a try every now and then. Good foods to incorporate with sex are: chocolate, strawberries, bananas, whipped cream, cherries, melons, ice cream, bacon, and champagne. Lick any of these off of your woman's parts.

Have her sit on your face:

This is incredibly sexy because it shows how close your partner is willing to get with you. Have her "sit on your face" and eat away! Have her move her hips up and down so she is giving you a face-rub with her pussy and butt.

Rim Jobs:

If you don't know what a rim job is-it is the art of sucking, licking, and kissing your partner's butthole. Rim jobs, if done right, can be seriously hot. Make sure your woman has showered previously (for obvious reasons.....). Have her sit in the "face down, ass up" position. Begin by devouring her pussy. Make sure to finger her vagina while licking away. Slowly begin nibbling and licking on her perineum (the area between her butt and pussy)." Continue to finger her clit during this time. Finally, kiss the area around her butthole, and then devour her butthole with your tongue. You can also spit on her butthole and rub the saliva from her butthole down to her perineum and pussy. This will all surely make her scream!

Chapter 4 – Rough Sex 101:

Don't stick to basic vanilla sex. Change it up! Rough sex does not need to be that "rough" but it is a great way to add kinks to your sex life.

However, make sure that both you and your partner consent. You don't want to be pulling your partner's hair or spanking your partner without their consent.

Here are the best rough sex tips:

Know your fantasies beforehand: Both men and women have their kinks and fetishes. Make sure that you and your partner discuss with each others fantasies first. If one of you has a particular fetish that the other one finds appalling, its important to know in advance.

Scream and yell: This intensifies the feeling and environment of your sex session. Make sure no one else can hear you though!

Nibble and bite (gently): This is great for erogenous zones such as the vagina, balls, penis, boobs, perineum, the butthole, the neck, belly, and inner thighs.

Claw your lover (again, gently).

Aggressive movements. Pounding and fucking each other aggressively like there's no tomorrow will turn you two on like nothing else.

Pulling each other's hair. Pulling your woman's hair while you are fucking her up her ass is dead sexy.

Slapping each other. A light slap across the face or your partner's butt is great for this.

Abusive dirty talk. Read my books on talking dirty for more about this! But saying to each other "fuck me like you hate me" or "call me a bitch!" are huge turn-ons.

Anal Sex: Although anal sex can be moderately painful for women, it is still hot. More women are wanting to give anal sex a try. Don't thrust too hard though!

Forcing your partner to perform sexual acts. For example, shoving your cock down your woman's throat is great for this. Sitting on your man's face and pressuring him to devour your pussy is extremely hot.

Spanking. Aggressive spanking, although can be moderately painful, can add some extra spice to your sex. It makes your woman feel like a pornstar. Ask her if she likes it when you slap her ass.

Light Choking: Grasping your hand over your lover's neck and gripping firmly (but not choking) is a fetish for many people because it reduces the flow of oxygen to the brain, creating a sort of dizziness.

Whipping: You can get a bdsm whip from a sex store. This goes in hand with submission. Show her she is misbehaving by whipping her!

Dominance and submission: Both men and women fantasize about either dominating their partner or being dominated by their partner. This is because it is extremely hot knowing that your partner can do whatever they want with you..... and you have no control over it!

Sex toys and gags.

Chapter 5 – Naughty places to have sex

Think about all the wildest and craziest places that you fantasized about having sex. Make it a reality! Relationship expert Emily Morse, Ph. D., says that expanding your sexual experiences outside of the bedroom leads to more spontaneity and more closeness with your partner. Great sex experiences are great for conversation with your partner and are great for making good memories with your partner.

Getting it on in different places is more about the new and exciting experiences you will have with your partner and not just about orgasm or ejaculation. By having new sex experiences in different places-you will learn more about yourself and what turns you and your partner on.

Many of the below locations are public-so use with caution!

Awesome place to have sex with your partner:

Your backyard: having sex in the backyard is a great place to get it on when you don't want to have to worry about getting caught but still want to do it outside.

The couch: fucking your woman on the couch with multiple pillows under your woman's back can increase the likelihood of orgasm.

Hotel Sex: A hotel has all the benefits of sex with none of the normal responsibilities of being an adult. You don't have to worry about making the bed or clean up-as housekeeping takes care of that. Plus-if you ever want to have crazy loud sex so that your kids won't hear-a hotel is a great place to go for an offsite fuckfest!

A public event: Weddings, sports events, parties, etc. This adds to the thrill of "we just might get caught." Definitely do this one when you want that excitement to be really high. Find a bathroom or a closet farthest away from the crowd.

If you only have a few minutes, this is a great opportunities to give her a quickie through her skirt-as this is easy to cover up if someone is coming!

Mirror Sex: Sex in front of the mirror is a huge turn on for women because she can see how she looks while jumping your bones.

On the Beach: This inherently is one of the most romantic places to have sex. However, make sure to do it on a towel-as you don't want sand getting in your vagina or butthole.

An Empty College Classroom or Library: This is a naughty one. Check the class or library hours to make sure you won't get interrupted. It is recommended that she wears a skirt or dress with no panties just to make the "in and out" easier.

A Park: Look for a beautiful park to do this on. Bring a tent or blanket with you!

An elevator: This one is naughty too and the risk of getting caught is high. However, its extremely hot. I would recommend saving this one for buildings or locations that aren't that busy. Make sure there isn't a security camera in the elevator!

A closet: Whether it be a party, event, or even at a friends house-fucking in a closet is hot.

A Jacuzzi: Book a room with a Jacuzzi if you don't own one. This too is one of the more romantic locations to get it on.

A limousine: This is great if you are having a limousine transport you somewhere and you can't keep your hands off each other during the ride. Make sure that the privacy window is down though.... Don't distract the driver!

A waterbed: This is a step up from regular sex in the bed. The slip and slide makes things rougher and more fun.

Private office party: If you have keys to a private office-show your partner how hard you work on that desk (in a different way).

A boat: Getting it on with waves in the background is awesome.

On a roof: This is still outside yet still gives you some privacy. However-don't be too loud!

The woods: It is beautiful to have sex where there is nothing but nature all around you. However, this is exciting and thrilling-because you never know if someone will walk by!

Chapter 6 – 35 Naughty Sex Games

Here are some more steamy games you and your partner can play!

Sex Game 1-The time bomb: For this game-set a time limit (10 minutes, 20 minutes, etc.) where you focus just on foreplay (i.e. kissing, touching, groping, teasing, etc.) for that period of time. However, no penetration or oral is allowed during this time

This game is great because it allows you to have a "pregame" before a wild sex session. Foreplay is critical!

Sex Game 2-Blind sex: Take a blindfold and keep on your partner for a period of time. This is hot for sex because this causes certain senses to be enhanced due to the lack of sight.

Sex Game 3-Prisoner sex: Tie up your partner (assuming he or she consents) to a position where they are submissive to you. You can use ties, ropes, or materials you can get from sex stores. Tie your partner up and do whatever you want with them!

Sex Game 4-Twister: Find a parking lot where no one else is. Have sex in the car in that parking lot. Make believe that your partner is a virgin. Give them step by step instructions on how to give you oral and how to have sex with you. This one is fun because it is a blast from the past, and also because it gives the two of you the opportunity to try new things!

Sex Game 5-Kinky Cards: Play cards and give each suit a sexual meaning, act, or position. Use a timer for, say, five minutes. When someone picks a particular suit, they either perform or receive that sexual act for five minutes.

Sex Game 6-Truth or Dare: Use this game as a way to find out more about your partner's sex fantasies and be more raunchy!

Sex Game 7-This is war: Get naked with your partner and have a pillow fight. Whoever surrenders first has to be submissive and do whatever sexual act the winner wants.

Sex Game 8- Fantasy Bowl: Each of you put your top ten sex fantasies on a small piece of paper and put them in a fishbowl. Talk about them together, why you think they are hot, and make them happen!

Sex Game 9-Role Playing: The man can pretend to be a doctor, and the woman can pretend to be the patient. The doctor can pretend he's examining the woman and use excuses to touch her in her erogenous zones. There are endless options for roleplaying. Use your imagination!

Sex Game 10-Would you rather?: Ask your partner dirty "would you rather" questions. This will get kinky and raunchy quick!

Sex Game 11-Strip Questions: Ask your partner some personal questions. If they get it wrong, have them remove an item of clothing and chug a shot of alcohol.

Sex Game 12-Sexy Dice: Assign a sex position to each dice. Once you role the dice and it lands on a certain number, perform the proper sex act on your partner.

Sex Game 13-Tarzan and Jane: Start out with the two of you in bed. The guy attempts to wrestle the girl, tie his girl's hands to the bed rest so he can penetrate her. The girl tries to resist. This game can be really fun. After a few minutes though, both the man and the woman will become really horny and it will lead to rough sex.

Sex Game 14-Blindfolds and food sex: This game requires ice cream. Blindfold your partner and give your partner a spoon. Have your partner attempt to feed you. If any of the ice cream drips on your body, they have to eat it off. In time they will be eating off in many places!

Sex Game 15-Reenact a porn scene: Watch a really horny kinky sex scene with your partner. Reenact every sex act exactly as in the scene.

Sex Game 16-Strip Pong: Play normal beer pong. Except once one of you scores, the other has to remove an item of clothing each time. The first one entirely naked loses, and has to give a sexual favor of the winner's choice.

Sex Game 17-One Step forward, One Step back: The woman lies naked in bed while the man stands at the door. He desperately wants to penetrate his partner. The woman asks him a question about her. If he gets it right, he gets a step forward. If he gets it wrong, he has to step back. He persists in this game until he makes it to the bed and gets some pussy!

Sex Game 18-Sports: While watching a sports game, you and your partner choose competing teams. When one team scores, the partner with the winning team gets to receive any sex favor from the other partner for five minutes.

Sex Game 19-Seven Minutes in Heaven: This is where the man locks himself and his woman in a small closet. He gets to do whatever he wants to sexually to his woman.

Sex Game 20-Sex toy hide-and-seek: hide sex toys around the house and have your partner find them. Once your partner finds one, they have to use it on you.

Sex Game 21-20 Kinky Questions: Have your partner ask you 20 questions to guess what your favorite sex fantasy is.

Ask questions like "Does it involve toys?" "Does it involve more than two people?"

Sex Game 22-Marco Polo: Next time the two of you are swimming in a pool alone-play Marco Polo. Once you two find each other-pull each others bathing suit bottoms off and get it on right there.

Sex Game 23-Orgasm rotation: Lie naked next to each other and play with each others' penis and vagina. Whomever comes first gives the other person oral sucking until the other comes. Repeat.

Sex Game 24-"Don't get caught" masturbation: Grope each other sexually in a public place such as a restaurant when no one else is watching. This adds to the arousal because you know that you might just get caught!

Sex Game 25- Mirror each other: Sit naked right in front of each other and starting kissing and licking each other. When one partner kisses or licks part of their partner, the other partner "mirrors" their actions and kisses and licks their partner in the same area.

Sex Game 26-Blindfold games: blindfold your naked man or woman. Then pour some chocolate sauce on your naked body. Your man or woman has to lean over and kiss and lick your body until he or she finds the chocolate with his or her tongue. Once they lick all the chocolate off of your body-rotate roles! It's your turn to put the blindfold on.

Sex Game 27-The "Try Not to Have Sex" Game: This game is good for building up sexual lust and sounds counterintuitive. You and your partner are both naked and continue to make out with each other. However, you both try to avoid having sex with each other. This avoidance ironically builds sexual tension. Once one of you gives in and attempts sex with the other-that person loses.

Sex Game 28-Slippery Steamy Sex-This is great when you and your partner either get out of a sauna or steam room. You and your partner will both have steamy bodies. This will make sex even hotter.

Sex game 29- Food oral: Take a scoop of ice cream and put it in your mouth. Then, give head to your man or lick your woman's pussy with the ice cream in your mouth. Warn your partner first-as it will give them a cold shock!

Sex Game 30- 30 seconds of pleasure: This encourages fast and aggressive sex. Have a timer for 30 seconds and let your partner do whatever they want to with you for 30 seconds. Once the 30 seconds is up-switch roles!

Sex Game 31-Spin the bottle: Spin the bottle, but instead of kissing-if the bottle points at you-you get to perform a sexual act on your partner of your choosing.

Sex Game 32-Sexy scavenger hunt: Make a list of all the sexy things your partner has to do and hide them around the house. Once he or she finds them-they perform the act on you.

Sex Game 33-Sex Monopoly: While playing a game of monopoly-instead of buying properties, "buy" pieces of your partner's clothes.

Sex Game 34-Body shots: This involves both of you being naked and using a dice, paper, and alcohol. Make a list of erogenous zones (boobs, pussy, perineum, etc.) and number them 1-6 on a piece of paper. When you role the dice, your pour the body shot on that area and lick/suck the alcohol off.

Sex Game 35-Be strangers: Agree to meet your partner at a bar, but pretend not to know each other. Make believe you are meeting for the first time, and engage in small talk. Once you "get to know" them, ask them over to your place and have the best make believe one-night stand of your life.

Conclusion

Thank you again for downloading this book!

I hope this book was able to help you learn some new moves to turn your boyfriend/husband or girlfriend/wife on.

The next step is to follow these tips and strategies to maintain an awesome and exciting sex life and physical relationship with your partner. Remember that this is more than just bringing lust back into the sheets. Instead, it's about communicating and affirming each other's value in the relationship.

Finally, if you enjoyed this book, then I'd like to ask you for a favor, would you be kind enough to leave a review for this book on Amazon? It'd be greatly appreciated!

Thank you and good luck!

Sexting Tips for Women:

100 tips to turn him on!

Check Out My Other Books!

Thanks for downloading my book! I am a firm believer that in order to have a fulfilling family life-one must be properly prepared and understand the fundamentals of relationships, how to be a good parent, and live an exciting and adventurous sex life. As you can see, I have written a series of multiple books on marriage, sex, and parenting. If you are looking to learn more about how to improve your marriage, sex and dating life, family life, etc.-please check out my other books! Simply click on the links below or search the titles below to check them out.

Parenting:

Parenting 101: 20 strategies to follow to raise well-behaved children

Raising Your Kids: Time Management for Parents for Stress-Free Parenting

Sex (General):

Sex Positions: Your Guide to the 50 Best Sex Positions for a sexy marriage!

Tantra Sex: The Beginner's Guide to 25 Tantra Techniques

Tantric Massage: Your Guide to the Best 30 Tantric Massage Techniques

BDSM Positions: The Beginner's Guide to 30 BDSM Techniques

Sex: Spice Up Your Sex Life! How to be maintain an awesome sex life with your partner and live your wildest sexual fantasies!

Sex Games: 35 Naughty Sex Games to make your Sex Life Hot!

Sex For Women:

Sexting: Sexting Tips for Women: 100 tips to turn him on!

Sex Positions for Women: The Ultimate Guide to the 50 Best Techniques to Turn Your Man On!

Talk Dirty: How to talk to get your man aroused and in the mood for sex!

Sex: The Hottest Tips for Better Orgasms!

Sex for Men:

Sex Positions for Men: The Ultimate Guide to the 50 Best Techniques to Turn Her On!

Dirty Talk: Talking Dirty for Men: 200 Examples to Get Your Girl Aroused and in the Mood for Sex!

Sex: Make her beg for more and be the best she's ever been with in bed!

Marriage:

Marriage and Sex: Why sex matters to keep romance alive!

Marriage for Women: Your Guide to a Happy, Fulfilling, Intimate Marriage!

Marriage for Men: How to be a good husband and have a happy, fulfilling, intimate marriage!

Marriage 101: How to have a long-lasting, happy and intimate marriage!

Wedding Planning: The Ultimate Guide to Budgeting and Planning your Wedding!

Marriage Communication: Your Guide to constructive praise, criticism, and communication for a happy, long-lasting marriage!

Divorce: Ten Steps to Preventing a Divorce and Save Your Marriage

Dating:

Tinder Dating: Your Guide to Creating a Strong Tinder Profile, Getting a First Date, and Being Confident!

Introduction

I want to thank you and congratulate you for downloading the book *Sexting Tips for Women*. I wrote this book in hopes that more couples would explore the option of sexting and dirty talk in their sexual relationships, as well as to clear up some misconceptions of dirty talk, and to provide just enough information to help make your man's as well as your, sexual fantasies come true.

This book contains proven steps and strategies on how to become a truly confident woman in the ways of talking dirty and sexting. It is time to wake up and start pleasing your man with those lips of yours, and I am talking about the ones on your mouth. Sheesh get your mind out of the gutter, there will be plenty of that later.

Here is a synopsis of what you will learn:

-Why foreplay is important to sex
-How to tease your man
-How to sext and how not to sext
-100 less naughty sexting tips
-100 much more naughty sexting tips

Chapter 1: Why foreplay is necessary (and downright sexy...)

For a massive ejaculation for your man and a massive orgasm for you-foreplay is a must! For women, it takes women a longer time to build up the necessary levels of arousal. Therefore, a slower and steady build up to orgasm is necessary. Foreplay prepares the body and mind for sex and makes the two of you hornier than if you simply walked right into sex.

Letting your man get in your pussy too easy is not good for orgasm. Do not rush through foreplay. Just like a runner needs to do a 10-15 minute warm-up before a long run-a couple needs to sexually tease each other and build up anticipation before a sex session.

Studies have shown that women need around 20 minutes of arousal time to reach the "orgasmic platform." Skipping the sex-response cycle makes it hard for men to ejaculate and cum and for women to orgasm. In the case of sex, patience pays!

You need to tell your man that foreplay is a must. Horny texts or sayings build sexual tensions. Both are little pick me ups and helpful ways to create sexual tension in the relationship. Foreplay also gives you more time, more options and in the long run makes it last. So guys why wouldn't you try foreplay?

Here are some basic foreplay tips:

Dirty Talk: I wrote two other books on this-but to summarize-men love women who do dirty talk. It is a huge turn on. Phrases such as "Pound my little wet pussy", "I want to lick, fuck, and suck your juicy sticky hard throbbing cock", "Bite my tits", or "I'm going to sit on your face and rub my wet pussy in your face" are huge turn-ons and great for foreplay.

Roleplay: I have an upcoming book on naughty sex-but to summarize exploring different roleplaying is a huge turn on. Dressing up like a slutty secretary or a sexy teacher is an awesome foreplay method.

Teasing: Gradually build up. You don't want to be giving head to a limp penis. Instead, as I always say-incorporate some foreplay first. Several minutes of groping, hand playing and making out are a great way to start. You can also kiss and lick his inner thighs several inches from his penis. This area is very sensitive and is a huge turn on.

Whisper something dirty in his ear: Tell him "I want your cock now!" real quietly in his ear.

Fondling: For no reason, grab his load or slap his butt. And don't ask for permission.

Chapter 2: How to tease your man sexually:

Playing a little hard to get along with some teasing is huge to success in the bedroom.

Here are some basic tips on teasing your man:

Attack him by surprise: An unexpected hug from behind or kiss will warm him up. Come up behind him, hug him, and then kiss the back of his neck. Squeezing his butt or slipping your hand down his crotch and graze against his cock will drive him nuts.

Make him work for it: In the middle of a make out session, put your hand on his chest and push him away moderately aggressively. Then move to the other end of the bed and say "come and get me."

Public Displays of Affection: Hold your man's hand while you two are walking. When sitting, have your hand on his thighs. If the moment is right, graze your hand over his package.

Touch: Some great places to touch your man are his forearms, his shoulders, thighs, lower back, and face.

Be naked more often: Being naked for no reason in your home or apartment is hot to your man.

Wear lingerie: Bending over near his face while you are wearing sexy slutty lingerie is hot. Pretend that you don't know that he is watching!

Play hard to get: Instead of simply saying "lets have sex tonight", say " I hope you behave well tonight!" or "I'm not sure if I'm going to spend the night tonight." Humans have a tendency to want what we can't have, which is why this builds attraction.

Compliment him sexually: Even telling him simply he looks strong, he's smart, funny, sexy, etc. are all still turn ons.

Wink at him: His mind will start to wonder what dirty thoughts you are thinking!

Brush against him: When walking by, "accidently" brush your hand past his butt. Or, if he is sitting on the couch, lean over and give him a kiss. "Accidentally" brush your boobs against his arm.

Release it: Too much teasing is a bad thing. Teasing without releasing is constant foreplay without and end goal. This will leave your man frustrated and impatient. Tease a little, then back off. Tease a little, then back off again.

Leave hints around him about sex: leaving a sex toy out in the open, or eating penis shaped food, or leaving some of your panties on the floor is great for this.

Chapter 3: Sexting 101

Sharing intimate information or showing some skin over the phone has become common and more risky these days. Approximately 32% of men and 38% of women regularly sext. That's a lot of naughty photos and messages being sent around the world! Sending steamy texts to your partner, if done right, can be a great relationship booster. Many people are more turned on by written words over phone and written erotica then they are by porn. Hence, you need to know how to do it right.

Here are your Sexting 101 tips:

Use sexting as foreplay: Sending your man a naughty message while you're at work is a great way to get him out of his head at the corporate grind and get excited to be home. Keep the texts short-but also keep them detailed, juicy, and graphic.

Be Kinky: When you remove all unnecessary barriers in sex communication-everything gets better. Couples who are open and horny in regards to their sexual desires have much more satisfaction in their relationships then couples who don't. Don't be afraid to be dirty with your partner! Life is too short to be perfect. Use a combination of playful talk ("I'm infatuated with how soft your lips are") and more raunchy, pornographic talk (i.e. "I want to swallow your hard cock," or "I want your tongue up my pussy").

Be careful about pictures: If you want to send your man any naughty pictures-you have to be careful. Due to the social media prevalence these days-you don't want that leaking out! However, if you send him any nude pics, make sure you don't show your face or anything that can reveal your identity and that the pic goes no higher than your boobs. You don't want your face on a nude body over the internet! With this precaution-if something leaks-at least no one will be able to tie a face to it.

If your man chooses to send you dickpics (which most women agree is not sexy), that's fine. However-make sure he understands that his face shouldn't be visible either.

Use a password on your phone: You do not want someone else's eyes on your steamy texts! Taking this precaution along with never leaving your phone unattended will eliminate the chance of someone else seeing anything.

Start out slow: do not get raunchy too quickly! This communicates to your man that you are too easy. Be playful and teasing at first. Once you've gotten to know your man for a longer period of time-then you can get to the more r-rated and x-rated texting.

Bring back a memory of his: This doesn't apply if the two of you haven't had sex yet. However, if the two of you had a horny experience that really turned both of you on-text him about it! For example "remember that time that you exploded cum in my mouth for 45 seconds? I can't handle myself. That was so hot." This will make him think back and want to repeat the past!

Ask him a dirty question: Asking him something to get him thinking of dirty things between the two of you is a huge turn on. For example "What would you do to me if I was wearing nothing but a trenchcoat at the front door?" spikes curiosity and fantasies in his head.

Compliment him: Men love being told how awesome they are. Tell him something like "you are making me so wet". Even something more PG works. Telling him you think he's hot and sexy is often enough too.

Do a sext strip tease: Show your man a picture of you fully clothed. Then send another with your bra and panties. Then remove the bra. Then the panties. However, remember to not show your face!!!

Sext him about your fantasies: If you aren't confident enough to tell your man in person about your fantasies-sext your man about them! Whether it be bdsm, threesomes, getting gangbanged, etc. I have a book titled "Spice up your sex life!" about this!

Chapter 4: Sexting Don'ts

Now that we've discussed how to sext-its just as important to figure out exactly how not to do it.

No childish talk: Don't say anything childish like "pee-pee" or "wee-wee." Use adult words. Cock would suffice much better. Get comfortable with using words like cock, pussy, tits, fuck, etc.

Don't do it too soon: Make sure you give yourself some time before you sext with someone. Many women have the habit of getting into it too soon. This communicates that it is too easy to get in your pants. Get to know your man's integrity first.

If you send a picture of your vagina to a man you barely know-you are in for a world of hurt. Too many leaks happen and don't think that it won't happen to you.

Don't store the photos on your phone: Save the photos elsewhere.

Don't sext the wrong person: Double check the phone number before you send the text message. You don't want your mom or dad to get a photo of your naked ass! That would make holiday dinners awkward.

Don't sext while drunk: You are very likely to make a sext that you will regret if you sext while drunk. You will likely sext the wrong person, too many people, or even post on social media. Definitely do not do this!

Do not wait too long to respond to a sext: Waiting too long kills the arousal. If your man sexts you but you don't sext back for 10 hours-chances are he will get busy with something else. He will likely not be aroused all day waiting to reply to your text.

Don't use emoticons: Emoticons are childish and take away the sex appeal. If they come up with blowjob, pussylicking, or anal sex emoticons-fine. However, for the most part you need to be mindful that for the most part these are childish and make the dirty talk less sexy.

Chapter 5: Sexting Examples (less naughty)

Now that we've given you some tips on how to and not sext- let's see how it is done in practice.

It is important that we distinguish between the less naughty and the more naughty texts.

Right below are some great sexts you can send your man to turn him on:

1. What are you wearing right now?

2. Are you alone tonight? Want to play a game?

3. I was thinking about you in the shower today.

4. I will see you in a while. I have got a sexy surprise for you.

5. I am wearing all red today, even the stuff underneath my dress.

6. What do you want me to wear later tonight?

7. Let's tease.

8. You and me, in the back of my car tonight?

9. When you are around, everything starts throbbing and it is not just my heart I am talking about.

10. I think your lips are really sensuous. I am talking about the ones I can see, you still have to show me the other one.

11. If you are tired then I can give you a massage tonight. Let me know where you want my hands to work the most.

12. Want to scream tonight? Stop by my place for a little while.

13. I sometimes feel like playing with your beautiful hair... and other things too.

14. You know how to push the right buttons.

15. Next time we see each other, I am going to show you what love is.

16. I do not need to watch porn anymore. One look at your sexy body keeps me going.

17. Why are your keeping me starved?

18. Next time when I am around you, wear something that keeps me guessing.

19. I want to take you to a place called orgasmland.

20. Want to see my '50 Shades of Grey'?

21. I am feeling very restless. Would you please come by and tie me up tonight? I will let you do whatever you want to do with me.

22. I want to force a few things on you tonight. Permission to be rough?

23. I will be your prisoner tonight.

24. Can I have my way with you?

25. If you could read my mind, you would start feeling really shy around me.

26. How can you turn me on so much just by looking at me?

27. What are your plans with me later tonight? Want to eat something delicious?

28. The next time you pass me by, I am going to tap it.

29. Your wardrobe needs to be updated. How about trying me on?

30. Let me be a part of your favorite fantasy?

31. I had a dream of you last night; you were mostly naked in it.

32. I can probably reach climax just by staring at your behind.

33. I got a whole new way to love you. Want to know what?

34. I feel like having some peaches and cream tonight, with you.

35. How about chocolate syrup all over?

36. What were you thinking yesterday when your hands were all over me?

37. I want to be naughty with you in the office.

38. Are your folks home tonight? I hope not. I do not want them to hear you screaming.

39. I have got a BIG surprise for you. It is in my pants and it will BLOW your mind.

40. Thanks to your skinny jeans, I already know how your behind would feel like.

41. I feel wasted just by looking at your pictures.

42. It gives me goose bumps just by thinking what will I do to your body.

43. Are you ready to go all night?

44. Did you tell me to 'come and get it' with your eyes last night?

45. Would you be my prey and I will be your hunter?

46. Would you like me to take you under?

47. My favorite thing on a dessert is whipped cream. Would you let me put it on you?

48. I know what you want and I think I am ready.

49. I got a plan for the both of us, but it involves my bed in it as well.

50. Just to let you know, I am a rider.

51. I have read some sexy things on the internet. Would you let me try it on you?

52. Why am I horny and you are so far away?

53. I think I need a doctor for this little love disease that I got. Would you please examine me from top to bottom?

54. I have got a new move. Will you let me show it to you later?

55. I have heard that you should not fight it, if you like it.

56. You left me turned on last night. Can you either switch it off or take it a bit further?

57. I really like your tie. Let us use it tonight.

58. Can you please save some energy for later, after you finish your gym? I have got a task for you.

59. I will let you frisk me if you will come and see me in next half an hour.

60. I will let you see mine if I will get to see yours.

61. Want to play tonight?

62. I have been thinking about some seriously racy stuff about you today.

63. You can look at it but you cannot touch it, YET.

64. Let us skip dinner tonight and eat something else.

65. We should stay in a hotel tonight. I am not sure if my neighbors would appreciate all the pounding noise and screaming.

66. I will follow you everywhere, as long as you will let me COME with you.

67. You have got a hypnotic cleavage. I do not think I can look at anything else but it, when we are together.

68. Your bulge is driving me mad.

69. Your dessert is HOT and READY for you.

70. Do you know if there is a way that I can resist those juicy lips of yours?

71. Why cannot I take your wet kisses out of my mind?

72. How will I be able to contain myself when I know that you are in the shower right now?

73. Did you think about me when you were in the bath tub today?

74. Just the smell of you gives me shivers.

75. I just looked at your picture on my phone and darling, you have sent my dial on high.

76. Let's get dirty tonight and wash it off each other in the shower later.

77. I am so much into you. I want to be in you.

78. I am thirsty, when can I see you?

79. I just want to feel your weight on me.

80. Would you let me ride you again?

81. Would you send me some pictures? Pictures you have not sent to anybody else.

82. Tonight in the club we will have our own dancing session, in a dark corner.

83. I have lost something. Would you let me look for it in your pants?

84. How about I come by to your office and you give me a tour of your insides?

85. I will pick you up by 8 o'clock tonight. Wear a skirt or a dress; my hands are a bit restless today.

86. It is really hot today, I think I am going to take my all my clothes off and just lay in my bed. See you in ten?

87. I have a JOB opportunity for you. Interested?

88. I was cooking something with lots of strawberries in it. I am covered in it now, would you come and lick it off me?

89. I am craving for you.

90. You are so kind to me. I am thinking of pleasing you all night tonight.

91. I am sending you this text with one hand, my other hand is busy. Come and join me.

92. You are going to be really exhausted by the end of the night tonight.

93. I want to serve you.

94. I want to kiss you so bad... all over.

95. I want to feel your strong grip on me.

96. All we are going to do tonight is teasing. Are you ready for the torture?

97. I am tired of sending you texts or speaking on phone. Why do not you come here and sit on the top of me?

98. How did you feel when I groped you in a public place last night... in my dream?

99. I am dripping with love and desire for you.

100.   Come on and soak me dry with that mouth of yours.

Chapter 6: Sexting Examples (very naughty)

Do not be afraid to use these. Be a brave, hot sexy woman and turn him on!

1. I love your ass in those jeans.
2. You make me wanna cum just looking at you.
3. You have the most amazing cock I have seen.
4. God I must have you now.
5. Rub my clit with your hard cock.
6. Your cock is stretching me out.
7. I want to feel every inch of your cock in me.
8. I want you to fill my pussy with that cum of yours.
9. Let me suck that cock, before you put it back in me.
10. Slap my ass harder
11. Finish on my ass.
12. Go slowly, I want to enjoy this.
13. Come make my pussy wet.
14. Shove that big cock in my ass.
15. I'm going to fuck you so hard.
16. Do you want to cum on me baby?
17. Do you want to fill my pussy with cum?
18. You are filling me all up baby.
19. Oh don't stop, not yet.

20. I want to make you moan and scream.

21. Say my name.

22. I've been very naughty, punish me.

23. That incredible, Fuck me again.

24. Tease me with your big throbbing cock.

25. Tell me how much you love it.

26. No one has even turned me on as much as you have.

27. Your body is so hot.

28. You are so sweaty.

29. Your penis drives me wild.

30. I want to ride you right now, so hard.

31. Let me get on top.

32. Let me rock your world.

33. Let me take the lead.

34. Do you want to punish me?

35. Do you want to make me scream?

36. Use those handcuffs on me

37. Cover my eyes, and get freaky.

38. Say my name when you do that.

39. I want to get naked with you right now.

40. Kiss me down under.

41. Do you like when I do that?

42. Do you like how that feels?

43. I love the things you do with your tongue.

44. I'm going to control you tonight.

45. I am going to make you my slave tonight.

46. You are the best lover I have ever had.

47. Show me what you can do.

48. Shut my mouth up with that big cock of yours.

49. Just lie back and let me make you cum,

50. You taste so good.

51. I want you so bad.

52. I'm so wet thinking of your rock hard long throbbing cock.

53. Oh I wish you were here so you could pound my little pussy.

54. I love it when you make me scream.

55. I want you to lick me all over.

56. I want to do so many bad things to you.

57. I wanna suck you like a lollipop.

58. Let's fuck in public.

59. (()) D====8

60. Tell me how bad you want it.

61. Tell me what you want to do to me.

62. Bend me over and use that pole.

63. Slam it in, I wanna scream.

64. Slap my ass, and pull my hair.

65. I want you to cum all over my face and tits.

66. I want to swallow your delicious cum.

67. I want you to fuck me till I can't walk anymore.

68. I need you now.

69. I miss you so bad, come here and give me a taste.

70. Just the tip.

71. Hold me down, and show me what you got.

72. I want you to choke me with that big cock of yours

73. I want to be gasping for breath, as I suck you off, and go deeper and deeper.

74. Oh I want you to make me cum.

75. I'm about to cum, I'm so close, oh right there yeah.

76. Lick me all over.

77. Lick my tits.

78. Get naked.

79. I've been thinking about you.

80. You were in my dreams last night.

81. Fuck me

82. Don't stop

83. 8====D

84. Faster

85. I'm almost there

86. Use your sperminator on me.

87. Use that dick of yours

88. I love it when I get you hard.

89. You are so hot.

90. Your muscles are bulging

91. I want that dick in me now

92. Your penis makes me wet.

93. I want to play with your balls.

94. Tell me how bad you want me

95. Oh you have me soaking wet, come in me and play

96. Be my little secret.

97. Make me cum in every room.

98. You got me wishing I knew you earlier.

99. Choke me with that cock of yours

100. I'm gagging on you, please don't stop.

Conclusion

Thank you again for downloading this book!

I hope this book was able to help you successfully learn to sext and how not to, and help arouse your man. I wanted this book to shed some light on the concept of sexting and why its important and be able to help with your relationship. Communication about all sexual desires is a must. Hopefully you have learned a few tricks, and are eager to please your man tonight! Don't forget the formula, and add your own flavor to it. Get creative, imagine no one else is in the room but you and him.

The next step is to experiment. Try out the formula, try out the tips, spice up your love life and make the next time you have sex an unforgettable experience. Use some of the examples on your man the next time you see him, and see his reaction. Always communicate no matter how awkward you might feel, you must be open and allow yourself to be sexually awakened.

With every awakening, it only takes one thing, or one time to be fully open to the possibilities. So give yourself to sex, spread those legs and let him in.

Finally, if you enjoyed this book, please take the time to share your thoughts and post a review on Amazon. It'd be greatly appreciated!

Thank you and good luck!

Talk Dirty:

How to talk to get your man aroused and in the mood for sex!

Check Out My Other Books!

Thanks for downloading my book! I am a firm believer that in order to have a fulfilling family life-one must be properly prepared and understand the fundamentals of relationships, how to be a good parent, and live an exciting and adventurous sex life. As you can see, I have written a series of multiple books on marriage, sex, and parenting. If you are looking to learn more about how to improve your marriage, sex and dating life, family life, etc.-please check out my other books! Simply click on the links below or search the titles below to check them out.

Parenting:

Parenting 101: 20 strategies to follow to raise well-behaved children

Raising Your Kids: Time Management for Parents for Stress-Free Parenting

Sex (General):

Sex Positions: Your Guide to the 50 Best Sex Positions for a sexy marriage!

Tantra Sex: The Beginner's Guide to 25 Tantra Techniques

Tantric Massage: Your Guide to the Best 30 Tantric Massage Techniques

BDSM Positions: The Beginner's Guide to 30 BDSM Techniques

Sex: Spice Up Your Sex Life! How to be maintain an awesome sex life with your partner and live your wildest sexual fantasies!

Sex Games: 35 Naughty Sex Games to make your Sex Life Hot!

Sex For Women:

Sexting: Sexting Tips for Women: 100 tips to turn him on!

Sex Positions for Women: The Ultimate Guide to the 50 Best Techniques to Turn Your Man On!

Talk Dirty: How to talk to get your man aroused and in the mood for sex!

Sex: The Hottest Tips for Better Orgasms!

Sex for Men:

Sex Positions for Men: The Ultimate Guide to the 50 Best Techniques to Turn Her On!

Dirty Talk: Talking Dirty for Men: 200 Examples to Get Your Girl Aroused and in the Mood for Sex!

Sex: Make her beg for more and be the best she's ever been with in bed!

Marriage:

Marriage and Sex: Why sex matters to keep romance alive!

Marriage for Women: Your Guide to a Happy, Fulfilling, Intimate Marriage!

Marriage for Men: How to be a good husband and have a happy, fulfilling, intimate marriage!

Marriage 101: How to have a long-lasting, happy and intimate marriage!

Wedding Planning: The Ultimate Guide to Budgeting and Planning your Wedding!

Marriage Communication: Your Guide to constructive praise, criticism, and communication for a happy, long-lasting marriage!

Divorce: Ten Steps to Preventing a Divorce and Save Your Marriage

Dating:

Tinder Dating: Your Guide to Creating a Strong Tinder Profile, Getting a First Date, and Being Confident!

Table Of Contents

Introduction

I want to thank you and congratulate you for downloading the book *Talk Dirty*. I wrote this book in hopes that more couples would explore the option of talking dirty in their sexual relationships, as well as to clear up some misconceptions of dirty talk, and to provide just enough information to help make your man's as well as your, sexual fantasies come true.

This book contains proven steps and strategies on how to become a truly confident woman in the ways of talking dirty. With 200 examples of dirty talk, and even a how to section, in which I will lay out the formula for you to create your own dirty talk, this book will become your sexual awakening. Let's face it dirty talk is taking over our world, you hear it in music, you see it in the movies all the time, and more and more people are beginning to use the option of sexting to improve their relationship. Well it is time to wake up and start pleasing your man with those lips of yours, and I am talking about the ones on your mouth. Sheesh get your mind out of the gutter, there will be plenty of that later.

You might think you can't learn to talk dirty, but you can. I will let you in on a little secret, the three key features a woman must have to talk dirty are; confidence, imagination and a sexual appetite. If you have all of these features, then talking dirty is like a walk in the park. Just follow these easy steps and soon you will be creating and acting out your man's every sexual fantasy.

Here's an inescapable fact: you will need confidence and a loving partner. If you want to make your love life stronger, more vibrant, and even a little spontaneous, then don't you dare put down this book. Read all the steps, confidence boosters, and little pick me ups along the way. . . You soon will be talking dirty in your sleep, and just maybe that will be a turn on for your man.

If you do not develop the skills of talking dirty, then please don't give up! Sometimes it takes a little extra time and patience to achieve the confidence and imagination to successfully talk dirty. You will be cumming along in no time ;)

It's time for you to become a confident woman with the capability of talking dirty at the drop of a dime. Next time you see your man, surprise him with a little dirty talk, and maybe he will reciprocate with something more. Don't get stuck into the same old routine, mix it up, go out, have sex on the kitchen floor, go crazy, but most importantly TALK DIRTY.

Chapter 1: Let's Talk About Sex

"Let's talk about sex baby. Let's talk about you and me. Let's talk about all the good things and the bad things that may be. Let's talk about sex. Let's Talk about Sex." -Salt N'Pepa

Why is it so difficult for some couples to talk about sex? I mean cum on! Sex is a healthy part of life, and should be enjoyed. Why are we still cowering in the corner every time it is mentioned? Why do we feel it is this disgusting action, and why are there so many misconceptions and arguments over it? Why? There doesn't need to be. It's time to talk about it.

Communicate to your man, tell him what you like and what you don't like. Don't assume he will know what to do if you don't tell him. I am sure he has no problem telling you what he likes and if he isn't speaking up, then let this be a lesson to you both. COMMUNICATE!

Sex isn't just for love, but it is also for pleasure. If you aren't doing it as much, or you no longer feel attracted to one another, then fix it. Make time, take time out of your day to tell your man how much he means to you. Try something new, don't get stuck in the same routine, and open yourself up to other possibilities. The possibilities are endless if you allow yourself to be sexually awakened.

Try something different, allow yourself to use your imagination and talk dirty. It is important for couples to talk dirty to one another once in a while, it keeps things fresh and exciting. I know many of you are thinking , only hookers and slutty girls talk to their man that way, but newsflash this is the 21st century if you want to sext your man during your lunch break, then go right ahead or if you want to text him a dirty little message late at night, then what is stopping you?

Talking dirty is becoming more and more popular as time goes on. It seems there are even more ways to talk dirty than before. You could use your phone, laptop, tablet, Facebook to IM him, or the good old fashion, face to face technique.

Here are some favorites of mine that are sure to get you on his mind. There will be 200 examples throughout the book, so keep a look out as the numbers increase ;)

1. I want you so bad.

2. I'm so wet thinking of your rock hard long throbbing cock.

3. Oh I wish you were here so you could pound my little pussy.

4. I love it when you make me scream.

5. I want you to lick me all over.

6. I want to do so many bad things to you.

7. I wanna suck you like a lollipop.

8. Let's fuck in public.

9. (()) D====8

10. Tell me how bad you want it.

11. Tell me what you want to do to me.

12. Bend me over and use that pole.

13. Slam it in, I wanna scream.

14. Slap my ass, and pull my hair.

15. I want you to cum all over my face and tits.

16. I want to swallow your delicious cum.

17. I want you to fuck me till I can't walk anymore.

18. I need you now.

19. I miss you so bad, come here and give me a taste.

20. Just the tip.

21. Hold me down, and show me what you got.

22. I want you to choke me with that big cock of yours

23. I want to be gasping for breath, as I suck you off, and go deeper and deeper.

24. Oh I want you to make me cum.

25. I'm about to cum, I'm so close, oh right there yeah.

26. Lick me all over.

27. Lick my tits.

28. Get naked.

29. I've been thinking about you.

30. You were in my dreams last night.

31. Fuck me

32. Don't stop

33. 8====D

34. Faster

35. I'm almost there

Those are just a few, but you catch my drift.

Chapter 2: Awkward Turtle
How to not be awkward when talking dirty...

Talking dirty is a skill, so it might take lots of time to perfect it. In the beginning you will most likely feel awkward, turn red, blush or even giggle. You need to be able to get that awkwardness and laughing sensation out of your system.

So how do you get that awkwardness and push it aside, so you can finally awaken? My first suggestion is to be naked. Seems like a silly suggestion, but studies show being naked more helps you appreciate your body and become more comfortable in your skin. After a long day of work, just go upstairs, strip down, look at yourself in a mirror and say "I am a confident, beautiful woman, who will show her man a whole new side of her." Do this 3 times a week, or every day if you want. Do it for as long as you need.

If being naked isn't something you want to try, then maybe communicate to your man. Explain how you are trying something different, and to keep an open mind. Tell him that you are going to rock his world. Men always love hearing that.

To get rid of possible giggles, watch a horror movie right before you are about to talk dirty, or get yourself in a real serious manner. Honestly, I think the laughing, and the awkwardness is all related to lack of self-worth and confidence. I know you have all heard of the saying "You need to love yourself first before you can love anyone." This rings true to talking dirty. How can you feel comfortable saying such vulgar things, when you aren't even comfortable with yourself?

Make sure you are comfortable, confident and imaginative when you begin. I will be having a chapter on What Not to Do with Dirty Talk, but that will be closer to the end of the book. I will give you a sneak peek here though...

Whatever you do, don't say something that offends you or your man. Turning your man on does not have to be degrading. You know what I mean, don't let him do things that you aren't comfortable with or upsets you. If talking dirty brings out a side of him you have never seen, make sure you lay down boundaries.

One woman I spoke with told me her boyfriend got so into the dirty talk that instead of having vaginal sex, he did anal and didn't let her know. Imagine that surprise! Ouch! Needless to say that night didn't end well, and it makes sense why. She wasn't comfortable with that type of sex, and maybe even told her boyfriend she never wanted to do anal, but it happened. Just imagine that night. So remember always say things you mean and intend to do, so you can avoid the above scenario.

I bet he was feeling like an awkward turtle. Don't let your dirty talk become awkward, keep it simple, sexy, and creative.

Chapter 3: Start Your Engines

Dirty Conversation Starters

Isn't it strange how the older men get the more difficult it is to start them up? Seriously, in high school, all over you, college, a fuckfest for sure, but marriage, not a lot of sexual activity on the radar. Plus you've seen the commercial for erectile dysfunction, how could you not? I swear they run that commercial into the ground. Doesn't matter what I am doing, eating dinner, cleaning, or writing, there it is that commercial. A commercial that has forever stained the male ego.

So how can you get your man in the mood? Now, I mean in the mood for anything; dirty talk, sex, or foreplay. How? I ask you, how.

One fun strategy is to use penis shaped food. There are plenty of options, and look bananas are even considered an aphrodisiac! Or what about a nice long hot dog, that you can put in and out of your mouth. A Popsicle even, a spoon, a straw, etc. The possibilities are endless.

With your imagination and creativity you can make anything sexual. You can start to get your man thinking about sex and dirty talk with just a lick of your lips. The real secret is, you have the power. You can make your man hang on to your every word, make him jump at the chance to have sex with you, make him start to talk dirty more and more often. Never forget that. The power is in your hands,

So next time you are at the mall with your man, if you are feeling pretty spontaneous, take the straw from your drink and suck it up and down. Not only will this action surprise your man, but it might make him reciprocate in words. Obviously he can't just take you in the food court, but you will definitely be on his mind. Being on his mind is the first way to start his arousal, the rest is up to him!

Chapter 4: Sexting Tips

How to talk dirty like a pro

This is the moment you have all been waiting for! This part of the book is the how to section in which I will give detailed instructions on how to talk dirty. I will give you a formula so to speak, and we will go from there.

First, you need to figure out how comfortable you are with what you are about to be saying. More simply put-know your limits. Do not say something if you have no desire to follow up with it. Do not say something if it offends you or him, or could be seen as degrading.

Second, know the environment you or your man are in. If you know he is at work, don't be sending dirty pics or dirty talk his way. His boss might see it, or he might get in trouble. If you know his lunch break schedule, then send it then. With all of these technological complications present, it is no wonder why most people do it the old fashion way of face to face. However, this chapter focuses on the technological aspects of talking dirty, so let's proceed.

Now dirty talk usually begins with a phrase, short, small and to the point. Maybe when you become more skilled, you can get more detailed, but for now we will stick to a few words.

Here is the formula: Begin with the word "your" then move to an adjective, then move to the body part, and end with an action. This is just a beginning exercise. 36) **Your throbbing cock makes me so wet**. You can change the formula up for instance instead of using the word "your" you could just say "I want" or "I need." So it could go like this 37) **I want your hard penis in me**.

You could also just say a few words to get your point across such as, 38) make me cum, 39) harder, 40) I'm so wet, 41) fuck me, 42)I want it now, etc.

Most importantly you should use your imagination. Using your imagination could make talking dirty more spontaneous and pleasurable. Use the same formula, but change it up. Maybe use more adjectives, or use a fun word to describe the body part. Here are some examples; 43) throbbing pole, 44) pitch that tent in my backyard, 45) snake, 46) the dicktator, 47) fuck puppet, 48) dong, 49) sperminator, 50) tonsil tickler, etc. Go wild.

Here are some more great examples:

51. I love your ass in those jeans.

52. You make me wanna cum just looking at you.

53. You have the most amazing cock I have seen.

54. God I must have you now.

55. Rub my clit with your hard cock.

56. Your cock is stretching me out.

57. I want to feel every inch of your cock in me.

58. I want you to fill my pussy with that cum of yours.

59. Let me suck that cock, before you put it back in me.

60. Slap my ass harder

61. Finish on my ass.

62. Go slowly, I want to enjoy this.

63. Come make my pussy wet.

64. Shove that big cock in my ass.

65. I'm going to fuck you so hard.

66. Do you want to cum on me baby?

67. Do you want to fill my pussy with cum?

68. You are filling me all up baby.

69. Oh don't stop, not yet.

70. I want to make you moan and scream.

71. Say my name.

72. I've been very naughty, punish me.

73. That incredible, Fuck me again.

74. Tease me with your big throbbing cock.

75. Tell me how much you love it.

76. No one has even turned me on as much as you have.

77. Your body is so hot.

78. You are so sweaty.

79. Your penis drives me wild.

80.   I want to ride you right now, so hard.

81. Let me get on top.

82. Let me rock your world.

83. Let me take the lead.

84. Do you want to punish me?

85. Do you want to make me scream?

86. Use those handcuffs on me

87. Cover my eyes, and get freaky.

88.   Say my name when you do that.

89. I want to get naked with you right now.

90.   Kiss me down under.

91. Do you like when I do that?

92. Do you like how that feels?

93. I love the things you do with your tongue.

94. I'm going to control you tonight.

95. I am going to make you my slave tonight.

96. You are the best lover I have ever had.

97. Show me what you can do.

98. Shut my mouth up with that big cock of yours.

99. Just lie back and let me make you cum,

100.   You taste so good.

Sexting makes you feel more vulnerable, because you won't be able to see his reaction, but you will know he is thinking about you. Another thing is sexting is a less effective way of dirty talk. He can't hear how you are saying it, your tone, the speed, or even if you are doing actions as well.

Sexting is a fun sexy way to remind your man you are thinking about him. A little dirty text, he will be thinking about you all day long and wondering what you are up to. You will become his little mystery. So when you are talking dirty to your man, remember less is more.

Chapter 5: Foreplay Tips
Make it last...

I know a lot of women complain that men are never interested in foreplay. Men always go right to it, nothing more and nothing less. If only men knew how much they were missing out on, if they tried a little foreplay.

Foreplay does a lot more than you think, and is actually very similar to dirty talk. Both are little pick me ups and helpful ways to create sexual tension in the relationship. Foreplay also gives you more time, more options and in the long run makes it last. So guys why wouldn't you try foreplay?

There are several options for foreplay.

You could dress up, be different people for the night, or act out certain scenarios. Your man could be a convict, and you could be his hostage. Or simple ones like pretending to have an affair. Some people don't like going too extreme when it comes to foreplay, so I have a few more options for you.

Take time appreciating each other's' bodies. Caress his arms, penis, and slowly lick his shaft up and down. Don't neglect the balls. If anything the balls should be the main star when it comes to foreplay, because they are often neglected during intercourse. Cradle his balls, suck each one in your mouth, nibble a little, and don't forget to stroke. While you are caressing the balls, go towards the shaft and go up and down with your tongue.

Another option is to make the dirty talk a form of foreplay. For this to work you really need to work on your delivery. You need to focus on your tone, body language, and speed of delivery. You could say it really slowly, and take dramatic pauses. You could whisper it or say it in a raspy voice. While talking always caress either his shoulder, arms or hands. Make sure you are doing an action other than speaking when you are talking dirty. Don't talk too fast, slow the speed down, almost as if you are done talking but then start again. This keeps him on his feet and guessing. Make sure you are keeping eye contact for a little, but then look away to tease him and keep it playful. One thing to remember when talking dirty is to always keep it playful and fun, never too serious or too demanding.

Next time your man wants to jump right into the sack, suggest foreplay, or further more just whisper in his ears these words 101) "I want you now." You could say something else as well, this is just to get you started.

Here are some more examples to use:

102. You make me so horny, baby.

103. I love it when you nibble on my nipples.

104. Don't you dare cum, until I tell you that you can.

105. Lick every inch of me.

106. I love how fast your cock can get hard.

107. Your wish is my command.

108. Don't stop, till I tell you to.

109. Do that some more.

110. I am going to lick and suck you till you come.

111. I want to have those lips all over me.

112. Fuck me naughty boy.

113. You can have me anyway you want.

114. Keep touching me down there.

115. Finger me till I squirt

116. I love when you go down on me.

117. I love how you use your tongue

118. Use your mouth on me.

119. Don't tell me to stop.

120. I want to kiss you all over.

121. Get that cock ready for me.

122. Hold me down and cum all over.

123. You are so sexy.

124. You got me dripping wet.

125. You have me thinking of you every minute of the day.

126. You make me so weak.

127. You make me want to lick every part of you.

128. I want to suck those balls.

129. I want to feel those balls pounding my pussy.

130. Kiss me harder.

131. I love feeling your strong arms.

132. I love how you smell.

133. I love the taste of you.

134. I love your cum.

135. I love you so much.

136. Tell me you want it.

137. Tell me you like this.

138. Tell me you love me.

139. Why can't you see how wet you get me?

140. Keep fingering me, don't stop.

141. Don't forget my ass.

142. Keep pounding me.

143. I want to make you cum.

144. I want to exhaust you.

145. Never forget I made you feel that way.

146. I've never cum so hard.

147. I've never felt so wet.

148. I've never had such an orgasm.

149. Oh fuck, fuck me good

150. Use that tongue of yours.

151. Harder, faster, cum for me.

152. Keep doing that, I like it

153. Use that tongue like you mean it.

154. Keep me wet

155. Be forceful with me

156. Make me blush

157. Take me to fucktown

158. Only you can make me feel this way

159. Your cock feels so good in my hands.

160. I never want you to stop.

161. Let me take control

162. Oh you like putting that up my ass, huh?

163. You are gonna make me a cum pie.

164. Can I just worship you?

165. I want to play with your balls.

166. Tell me how bad you want me

167. Oh you have me soaking wet, come in me and play

168. Be my little secret.

169. Make me cum in every room.

170. You got me wishing I knew you earlier.

171. Choke me with that cock of yours

172. I'm gagging on you, please don't stop.

173. You are big as fuck.

174. You like that big boy?

175. Tell me just how much you want me

176. Kiss me like you mean it

177. You take my breath away

178. Explore my caverns

179. Use your sperminator on me.

180. Use that dick of yours

181. I love it when I get you hard.

182. You are so hot.

183. Your muscles are bulging

184. I want that dick in me now

185. Your penis makes me wet.

186. Tell me why you gotta be so good....

187. Don't tell me to stop screaming, I like it.

188.   Oh oh oh fuck that feels good.

189.   Cum for me baby

Chapter 6: Say What?!
What not to do with dirty talk . . .

So we have gone through why dirty talk is so important, many examples, the formula for it and even some helpful hints. However, one thing we really need to clarify is what not to do with dirty talk.

Dirty talk is a new focus to explore, but with every exploration you need to be careful. As already addressed earlier on, make sure what you say you follow up with. Nothing is worse than getting a guy excited, and then ending up with blue balls. Make sure what you say doesn't offend or bring up some kind of drama. Possibly what you say could be degrading to you, or even offend your man. Make sure you are comfortable with what you are saying. If you are not comfortable with what you are saying then don't say it. If you don't mean it, then what is the point? Just make sure to continue working on becoming more and more confidence. With confidence your dirty talking ability will really improve.

Another thing you want to make sure is that you dirty talk in appropriate environments. This was already discussed earlier on in the book, but should be repeated. Someone could lose their job if done in the wrong environment. You wouldn't want your man's boss reading a text you sent for his eyes only, and vice versa.

Another thing to keep in mind is talking dirty is a fun, and a flirty way of creating sexual tension. However, if you are always talking dirty, this won't be a surprise for your man anymore, so it will lose its appeal if you will. So you need to make sure that when you are talking dirty that you don't overdo it. If you keep doing it, then your man will begin to expect it, and then you will fall into the same old routine.

Don't laugh, or be awkward with your dirty talk. This will most certainly ruin the mood, and then you will be screwed-not in the good way. Don't say over complicated phrases, the point of dirty talk is to be short and to the point. No one wants to read a paragraph of porn, but a flirty little text like 190) "You make me so wet" with a winky face, now that kills every time.

Last but not least, make sure you have fun with it.

Conclusion

Thank you again for downloading this book!

I hope this book was able to help you successfully learn to dirty talk, and help arouse your man. I hope this book has made you feel more confident and comfortable in your abilities. I wanted this book to shed some light on the concept of dirty talk and be able to help with your relationship. Hopefully you have learned a few tricks, and are eager to please your man tonight! Don't forget the formula, and add your own flavor to it. Get creative, imagine no one else is in the room but you and him.

The next step is to experiment. Try out the formula, try out the tips, spice up your love life and make the next time you have sex an unforgettable experience. Use some of the examples on your man the next time you see him, and see his reaction. Always communicate no matter how awkward you might feel, you must be open and allow yourself to be sexually awakened.

With every awakening, it only takes one thing, or one time to be fully open to the possibilities. So give yourself to sex, spread those legs and let him in.

I'll end with a few more creative examples of dirty talk found in movies.

191.   "Take me to bed or lose me forever" (TopGun)

192.   "I want you inside of me" (Ghostbusters)

193.   " I wanna be on you" (Anchorman)

194.   "I'm glad he's single because I'm going to climb that like a tree" (Bridesmaids).

195.   "When was the last time you came so hard and so long you forgot where you are?" (Torchwood)

196. "How would you like to have a sexual encounter so intense it could conceivably change your political views?"(The Sure Thing)

197. "I don't make love. I fuck. Hard. (Fifty Shades of Grey)

198. "One day, lady superspy Susan Cooper, I will fuck you (Spy)

199. "Do I make you horny, baby?" (Austin Powers: International Man of Mystery)

200. "You must forgive my lips....they find pleasure in the most unusual places."(A Good Year)

Finally, if you enjoyed this book, please take the time to share your thoughts and post a review on Amazon. It'd be greatly appreciated!

Thank you and good luck!

Talking Dirty for Men:
How to Get Your Girl Aroused and in the Mood for Sex!

Check Out My Other Books!

Thanks for downloading my book! I am a firm believer that in order to have a fulfilling family life-one must be properly prepared and understand the fundamentals of relationships, how to be a good parent, and live an exciting and adventurous sex life. As you can see, I have written a series of multiple books on marriage, sex, and parenting. If you are looking to learn more about how to improve your marriage, sex and dating life, family life, etc.-please check out my other books! Simply click on the links below or search the titles below to check them out.

Parenting:

Parenting 101: 20 strategies to follow to raise well-behaved children

Raising Your Kids: Time Management for Parents for Stress-Free Parenting

Sex (General):

Sex Positions: Your Guide to the 50 Best Sex Positions for a sexy marriage!

Tantra Sex: The Beginner's Guide to 25 Tantra Techniques

Tantric Massage: Your Guide to the Best 30 Tantric Massage Techniques

BDSM Positions: The Beginner's Guide to 30 BDSM Techniques

Sex: Spice Up Your Sex Life! How to be maintain an awesome sex life with your partner and live your wildest sexual fantasies!

Sex Games: 35 Naughty Sex Games to make your Sex Life Hot!

Sex For Women:

Sexting: Sexting Tips for Women: 100 tips to turn him on!

Sex Positions for Women: The Ultimate Guide to the 50 Best Techniques to Turn Your Man On!

Talk Dirty: How to talk to get your man aroused and in the mood for sex!

Sex: The Hottest Tips for Better Orgasms!

Sex for Men:

Sex Positions for Men: The Ultimate Guide to the 50 Best Techniques to Turn Her On!

Dirty Talk: Talking Dirty for Men: 200 Examples to Get Your Girl Aroused and in the Mood for Sex!

Sex: Make her beg for more and be the best she's ever been with in bed!

Marriage:

Marriage and Sex: Why sex matters to keep romance alive!

Marriage for Women: Your Guide to a Happy, Fulfilling, Intimate Marriage!

Marriage for Men: How to be a good husband and have a happy, fulfilling, intimate marriage!

Marriage 101: How to have a long-lasting, happy and intimate marriage!

Wedding Planning: The Ultimate Guide to Budgeting and Planning your Wedding!

Marriage Communication: Your Guide to constructive praise, criticism, and communication for a happy, long-lasting marriage!

Divorce: Ten Steps to Preventing a Divorce and Save Your Marriage

Dating:

Tinder Dating: Your Guide to Creating a Strong Tinder Profile, Getting a First Date, and Being Confident!

Introduction

There are plenty of reasons why couples need to talk dirty to each other. But the top one would be because the both of you need to know what the other person is comfortable doing. Let's say that there is a sex position that one person wants that they have never tried before. If they are to ever get their partner in the mood to give it a shot, they are going to have to be open and honest about their desires, and not be afraid if their partner is hesitant. But there is no way to know how comfortable they are or will be unless you voice it.

It's always going to be to your benefit to keep your partner aware of what is going on. Surprises are good, but not always. You don't want to sneak something in on them that they are not ready for just because you think it is sexy, and that goes for women as well as men. But this book is for the fellas, so it's important to know guys that one bad decision could mean the difference between a night of passion and you ruining the mood. Keeping your lover in the loop with great dirty talk is what the following chapters are all about. There will be 200 examples of dirty talk numbered throughout the book, so watch as the number increases. Enjoy!

Chapter 1: Why Couples Need Dirty Talk

When you talk dirty in bed, it brings about spontaneous ideas that you never thought were there. Simply living in the moment can spark up something new and fresh that you didn't even think was available. The moment the sensual words leave your lips the chances of your creative juices starting to flow increases greatly. But believe me, if the moment is hot enough, those are not the only juices that will begin to flow, and as you and your partner begin to trade off ideas you'll realize that you really aren't planning anything at all...it'll feel natural to talk dirty.

Probably one of the best reasons to talk dirty in bed is because it is wonderful for foreplay. Sure, there may be other ways that you do it for your partner, especially if you know them and have been together for a long time. You know where to touch them to make them hot, but if you choose the right words at the right time there will be an increased intenseness that you weren't aware of before. Choosing the right words can make an already hot foreplay routine ten times better.

When you aren't afraid to talk dirty to your partner, and really open up, you'll see a side of you that you didn't before. Your words will be coming from a place that is not planned or proper or grammatically correct, or anything near what you can say in public. You will be saying exactly what you are doing or want to do right in the moment, and you will undoubtedly at some moments surprise yourself. This is especially true if you have just started to experiment with talking dirty. You may end up going into a direction that you never imagined with your partner.

The key to talking dirty is to give it an element of surprise. Although you should not surprise your partner with an actual act without explaining first, you can always safely surprise them with your words. The key is to not overdo it when you are not in bed, because it could take away from the intimate moments between the sheets. Don't bed-talk in the car, in the kitchen, or anywhere else public, unless of course you and your partner are adventurous and are purposefully trying to arouse yourselves in these places. I'm not telling you to have sex in public, although some do find it quite erotic!

Talking dirty in bed will always lead up to better sex. What's the best part about it is you do not have to master it to make it work for you. In fact, when you say exactly what's on your mind, some of the funniest things will come out of your mouths, and you'll sometimes find yourselves laughing out loud as you challenge each other to go back and forth saying the dirtiest lines the both of you can think of. Sex is supposed to be happy, and you'll see just what I mean when you find that talking dirty is a much needed thing.

Chapter 2: Talking Dirty Without Feeling Awkward

Sometimes the reason some people don't talk dirty is because they just feel really weird doing it. They aren't used to actually saying what they want although there is no doubt in their mind that they want it. There are a few ways that you can get better at it if you feel that you could use some guidance. But you will soon find as you read on that there is no really perfect way to talk dirty. The biggest steps are figuring out when to do it and what you find are the biggest turn-ons for your partner.

One thing you should never do is try to be something or someone that you are not when talking dirty. I want to be clear on this point, though, because there are those couples out there who roleplay. If you are in character, then yes, go ahead and play your role and be someone that you are not! But if you are not actually acting out a character and being extra kinky that day, then it is always best to not come across as fake. Be yourself, and talk to them when you say dirty things that reflects your natural tone of voice, especially if you are whispering it in their ears.

When you remain honest, the natural way you feel will come out and your partner will feel that you are being genuine and real when you say the things that you do. It is not good if your words come across as forced – it will make it look like you are *trying* to talk dirty instead of simply talking dirty. For example, you could repeat a scene from the night before sometime when she won't expect it the following day. When you feel she is not thinking about it, walk over to her and whisper how you loved one certain thing she did in bed. Repeat the scene to her.

You don't always have to wait until it is time for sex to talk dirty. For example, there are always times during the day where you could call your partner and make them aroused with a few words. Or you could text her a few times with things like 1) I can't wait to walk through the door so I can go down on you again..."or 2) Does your pussy tickle your legs when you walk? This will have her thinking about the evening to come, and anticipation always heightens the pleasure.

One little trick when talking dirty is to use the word "I" a lot. When you do, it lets the woman know that it is your desire for her to do the thing that she did again. 3) I like it when you... or 4) I want you to.... or 5) I just love it when you... The things you specify are going to stand out in her mind simply by you using the word "I" consistently in your dirty talk. Be sure to use it in a balanced way, though, because you want to know what she wants as well.

When you talk dirty to your partner, it lets her know that you are thinking of her, and desire for her. Women are emotional, and want to know that she is always on your mind. She needs to realize that she is special, and one of the ways to do that is to focus your energy on keeping you on her mind. This way, not only will she slowly be aroused throughout the day, but she will also eventually become more open about trying things with you even, if she did not previously before.

But still, it's important not to put way too much pressure on yourself when it comes to talking dirty. Confidence wins, and if she is kind of shy she'll still follow your lead if you feel comfortable. For example, if you and she were sneaking in a quickie in a place where you could possibly get caught, the thrill and exhilaration would make her want to make love there with you, but as the man you have to remain confident in those moments. It could mean the difference between your erotic episode happening or passing you by.

Chapter 3: Foreplay Tips

Okay, let's get into the tips for foreplay. Among the most requested things that women want guys to do is pay more attention to their boobs. I know, it was a shock to me as well. What guy doesn't just love a nice set of boobs, right? Well, as it turns out, many fellas don't pay enough attention to them during foreplay. It's important to remember that your lady needs to feel sexy herself when slowly building up to sex. That being said, she wants you to play with them more. Take more time to squeeze them and nibble them, and she will definitely appreciate it.

The next thing to remember is to be gentle during foreplay. The way to do this is to simply slow down. You can do what you have planned, but the entire purpose of foreplay is to take your time to be sensual. So, remember to always be soft to the touch. Sometimes guys will be too aggressive with their fingers, for example, around her clit. It turns her on a lot more when you do it slower. Not just finger action either. Everything from kisses to rubs across her body should be done extra slow. It will make your time together that much more special to her if she knows that you are there with her in the moment every step of the way.

Putting on slow music usually helps as well if you have trouble slowing down on your own during foreplay. If she likes smooth jazz you could turn that on for background music, or some sexy R&B. The vibe will change as you play slower music, and you will almost naturally do things like rub and kiss her at a pace that she can really feel. This type of foreplay relaxes her enough so that she can climax when it is time.

One of most complained about things by women as well is also a part of foreplay that should always be followed by guys. Fellas, don't be in such a rush for the end result that you forget to do the one thing that she really wants you to do – undress her. It is a little disappointing to her when she has to take her own clothes off. So again, depending on if she wants rough sex or slow and sensual will determine how aggressively you remove her clothes...just go with the mood.

When you use your tongue during foreplay, it is one of the sexiest things you could do. But, you should not overdo it, whether you are kissing her lips or otherwise. For example, there are not many women who don't absolutely love neck kisses. But although you can use a little tongue here, there is no need to slobber all over it. Too much tongue can be nasty, especially if you are around her ears. A light kiss and lick is okay, but don't make her think that you are trying to clean them for her.

Another mistake women complain about is if we don't use both of our hands during foreplay. For example, if you are going down on her, then you may use both hands for a few minutes in the beginning, but then you will have a free one. The key is to not be lazy. While you are using one hand down low, use the other one to touch her all over her body. Caress her breasts, rub her thighs and her legs. The touch coupled with your clitoral stimulation will make her that much more excited, and the chances of both of you climaxing increases greatly.

Foreplay is about multitasking, if you will. For example, let's say that you are in a missionary position on top and are fingering her. Don't hover over her staring, kiss her simultaneously. She wants you to feel like you are all over her body, and that can be hard to do when you are only focusing on one thing at a time. Multitasking only gets easier and easier as you get to know her better and better, and can even end up leading to new things to try during foreplay. The two of you will continue to evolve as time goes by.

Performing well during foreplay with your lady has a lot to do with doing what you are already supposed to do. How many times have you heard your lady complain about things that have nothing to do with sex, such as you not paying attention to her completely? It's funny, but if you are on the couch with your girl and watching the game and ignoring her, she will likely tell you so many things about yourself that you don't do just to get your attention. Again, one of these things is not noticing when she is trying to do something for you, like wear sexy lingerie.

As men, the minute we see our lady in lingerie we want to commence ripping it off. But, during foreplay, you have to take those moments to take it all in. She put in a lot of time and energy picking it out and couldn't wait to show you how good she looked in it. So, that being said, you need to be prepared to compliment her in some way when she gets up and walks around. Sometimes all you have to do is make sure she sees you staring at her. When she catches you looking, that's when you give her the compliment.

One more thing about foreplay that I have to stress. You need to nibble, not bite. Just as with the tongue too much can be bad, the teeth are the same way! She likes it with a little nibble, not something that will result in teeth marks on her body! Speaking of marks, hold off on the hickies as well. If she likes them, then be sure to do it in inconspicuous places so that the folks at her job the next day don't stare at her during her shift.

Chapter 4: Sexting

Without a section on texting, many of you would be lost, because the majority of communication today is over via messaging. In fact many people text more than they talk with their real voice on the phone. So, that being said, when trying to practice how to talk dirty, texting (or sexting) is in your bag of weapons and tricks. There are certain ones that I will point out that are the most effective, but you are always free to experiment with ones of your own. Some of the ones I mention you will realize that you have used before and didn't even know you were sexting!

It's only right that I start off with one that is so natural that it was popular way before text messages became sext messages. When you inquire about what she has on, it makes her feel as if you are imagining about her right then and there, which you are. When you start off sexting with this line, she will be curious as to what you will say next. You can never go wrong with the sext message 6) What are you wearing? As she begins to describe her clothes to you, it is likely she is already following your lead.

Now, once she gets done with describing what she has on, she will sometimes ask you what you are wearing. Even if she doesn't, you still want to have a back-and-forth dialogue going on, or an in-and-out dialogue, if you will. Describing your clothes to her whether she asks you to or not will let also give you a chance to compliment her, as you should always do when she describes her clothes to you. The exchange of information can be super erotic even in the beginning of the conversation.

Now that you have talked about clothes, the next message you send should hint on something that has nothing to do with clothes – in fact this message will reflect the direct opposite.

You want her to know that you are aroused by her, so you now need to paint a picture in her mind that shows you thinking of her in your private thoughts. You will likely make her smile if you send her a text message telling her that you were thinking of her in the shower that day, or the night before. The shower is intimate, and she'll respond accordingly.

Sexting can also be funny. In fact you will find more funny ones than anything. Being that you are not physically there you want her to have this type of reaction every few messages - a laugh out loud moment. The rest of them should be a little nastier in between the funny ones. A good rotation of messages would be to send two or three private and very sexy ones, then one that is sexy and funny allowing her to laugh every few messages. This way you don't go so deep and keep the sexting fun yet very enticing.

So let's do a quick rotation of sext messages...three very sexy ones and one laugh out loud one. You could start off with 7) You have my heart **and** my pants throbbing right now... Then you could continue with another hot sexy one such as 8) I love your lips...when do I get to see the other set? Then do another one like 9) You turn me on each time you look at me... Then, say something really funny but sexy like 10) I'm texting with this hand but my other one is busy...can you help?

Here are some more fun ones to try on your girl tonight!

11)   You are making me so hard, thinking of your rockin bod.

12)   Oh are you wet baby?

13)   I wish I had my hands all over you.

14)   I can't stop thinking about you.

15) Remember last night, when you went down on me...

16) I want your body now.

17) I want to lick you all over.

18) Let me suck all those juices right out of you.

19) I wanna titty bang you!

20) Let me suck on those nipples.

21) Send me a naughty pic.

22) Oh baby you got my dick begging for it.

23) No one else can make me as hard as you can.

24) Let me see you naked.

25) Do you know what I want to do to you right now?

26) What are you thinking about?

27) Let me please you baby with my lips and nothing else.

28) I want to make you cum so hard.

29) Let me feel you.

30) Oh baby are you getting wet for me?

31) Tell me how much you need me right now.

32) I wanna make love on the beach.

33) You got me losing my focus.

34) I want to eat that ass.

35) I want you to suffocate me with your lips, and not the ones on your face .

36) I wanna finger bang you baby.

37) I am gonna rub your clit so good, you will be begging for me to keep going.

38) I am gonna tease the fuck out of you tonight.

39) I wanna rip off your clothes.

40) Let me fuck you hard.

41) Tell me what you want.

42) Don't be shy baby.

43) I am gonna make you scream.

44) I am gonna choke you with my big dick, but you are going to like it.

45) I am gonna fuck you on the kitchen floor tonight.

46) What kind of panties are you wearing?

47) You wearing that cute little lacy bra right now?

48) I want to rip your clothes off with my teeth.

49)   I want to unsnap your bra.

50) Let me love you.

Once you get used to sexting, it will get more and more fun. Sexting is actually a kind of foreplay, being that everything you say can lead up to the ultimate climactic period by the time you actually see one another. Some people say that there is a limit to what you can say on a sext, but depending on how long you have known your partner the phrases you use can have no boundaries. Still, obviously if you just met her you will want to start off with light stuff and gradually work your way up.

Chapter 5: Examples of Dirty Talk

Okay, okay. I know many of you readers are saying to yourself "Enough playing around...can you just give me some stuff to say?!!" I saved this section for last because lots of folks just jump to the things to say and not pay attention to the other important rules of dirty talk in the chapters before. But, if you have paid attention this far you are now ready for the best phrases to use when talking dirty. There are three levels that you need to be able to separate when doing it: the Taming Level, the Dirty Level, and finally the Filthy Level.

The Taming Level is mostly words that you would use to warm up to her. These are the type of phrases that you would use to initiate foreplay. They should always be suggestive in nature, and very flirtatious, but no more than that. You want to tease her with these types of phrases, and make her want you just as much as you want her. Sometimes it may be hard to stay within this territory, but you need to, especially if you just met her. You have to balance your dirty talk adequately.

The second stage is the Dirty Level. This level is in the middle, so you have to be sure to stay in the right zone and not talk too lightly or heavily. At this point you can actually let your hormones take control a little more, and transfer those feelings into words. You will be able to be as open as you need to be to get to that next level, and if you do it right you definitely will. That next level that I am referring to, of course is the last one, the Filthy Level.

Truth be told, many women like to hear the filthy level all the time, then there are others who never want it. When you reach this level, nine times out of ten you have known this woman for a long time, and you and she have already been intimate, probably many times before. This level is for when you want to get really freaky and kinky with your words for her, and many times this dirty talk is used only during sex or immediately before. Either way, if you have made it to this level with her than she is likely going back and forth with you with her own dirty talk already.

What I will do is give examples of each level from the lowest to the highest for the remainder of this chapter. This way you can process the information gradually, and get a feel for the level that you need to take right now with the woman that you like and want to start talking dirty to. If you don't want to say curse words, then you are not going to be able to talk dirty on the highest levels. But, if you don't mind saying a few to get her aroused, then here we go.

The Taming Level

Women love compliments, so you can always start off by telling her how good she smells. Smell is the strongest sense tied to memory, so that's why women are very particular about the scents they wear. She will love it when you notice it. Next you could tell her that you have been thinking about her all day, all week, etc. When she knows that she's been on your mind that long, then she will definitely smile, or respond in a positive fashion.

From there you want to give her compliments about her body...

51)   Oh my God you have a sexy waist...

52)   Damn, girl you have a nice figure...

53)   God broke the mold when he made you.

You want to make her blush at this point, and these are a few body comments that will help you develop more of your own. To go a little further, you could whisper in her ear in a public place...

54)   You know what? I can already taste you on my tongue and lips...

You could use that one if you are about to go down on her as well, but there is something about whispering it to her that makes her panties heat up. You could also use these;

55)   I wanna wrap my arms around you.

56)   You are perfect in every way.

57)   God must have forgot you were an angel.

58)   How can you be so wonderful?

59)   You make me blush just thinking of what I'd do to you.

60)   Girl, you are my everything.

When you compliment her body at this level, how long you have known her will determine what part of her frame you say things about. You would complement her face and clothes if you don't know her that well, but if you are spontaneous and feel comfortable you can tell her...

61)   You have a sexy-shaped ass...

62)   Your legs are so sexy...

Use the word "sexy" a lot, no matter how long you've known her. The keyword in it is "sex", and no matter how gentleman-like you approach her, the goal is still to get her aroused.

63)   Damn, your lips are sexy....

64) That is one sexy outfit...

65) It's a crime to be that sexy, girl...

66) Call the police, this girl is too hot to handle.

67) You are so beautiful.

68) Damn you sexy!

69) That top gives good cleavage.

70) I love the curves of your body.

71) Is that shirt new?

72) I can see your bra through that top honey.

73) I wanna lick inside your panties.

If you are in a relationship you can say

74) You wanna know something? Tonight you are mine...

That one is good if you live together, so is...

75) Damn, baby, you have me all turned on...

Make sure she knows that you have had her in mind with

76) Baby if I told you all of the nasty things I've been thinking about you all day long....

77) If I told you how long I've waited for you...

78) I've been thinking of your tits all day long.

79) Your perfect ass has been on my mind since this morning.

80) Tonight you do what I say.

81)   Let me please you.

82)   I've never stopped thinking about you.

83)   I've had your taste in my mouth all afternoon...

84)   Damn you have me so fucking hard right now....

85)   Hold me like you'll never let me go.

86)   Give yourself to me.

87)   I will satisfy you.

88)   I will turn your world upside down.

89)   Tonight, it is all about you and me.

90)   Let's make some magic.

91)   Let me make you happy.

92)   I will tell you everything.

93)   I want to pleasure you all night long.

As you can see, we are beginning to get into the next level of talk. Make her wet even if she isn't by saying to her

94)   Look how wet you are getting...

Even if she has on all of her clothes she will begin to feel it. Use that one at the right moment. Also, use ...

95)   I am going to make you scream...

96)   I'm gonna have you spelling my name baby...

97)   I'm gonna make the neighbors hear you screaming my name...

98)   I'm going to make your thighs shiver when you cum...

99) I am gonna make your lips shake.

100) Oh you are dripping all over me baby.

101) I like that feeling baby.

102) Let me touch you.

103) I am going to have you fucking like a pro.

104) Hmm baby, I love the taste of you.

105) Fuck, I love it when you are wet.

106) I love the feeling between my fingers.

107) You smell so good babe.

108) Look how hard you have me.

Okay, let's move on.

The Dirty Level

Alright. If you have gotten to this point you are in good shape as far as getting her aroused goes. Now all you have to do is use the correct lines to keep it going. The last section was pretty clean being that is was simply for taming. But remember when I said that there would be curse words on the way? Well, from here on out potty-mouth just doesn't describe good enough what you are about to become. Remember, this is not the section to start out with, so if you skipped the other ones go back, right now! ☺

To make it simple, this shit is stuff you will say when you are already hitting the pussy. In fact, you can build from these on your own, she will definitely come back with her own phrases.

109) Fucking right...take that dick, baby...

When she is letting you go deep inside of her...

110) Damn that shit feels so good....

111) Your pussy is the perfect fit for my dick...

112) Your pussy feels like waterfalls.

113) Bounce on that dick, baby...

114) Damn you one sexy ass bitch...

115) Who is my sexy little bitch?

You can change bitch to "girl", "slut", "thing", or whatever else she may be into.

Go ahead and ask her how she feels as well.

116) Do you like the way I stroke that pussy?

117) Can I go deeper baby?

118) You want it slower or faster?

119) Whose pussy is this?

While you're having sex, you can also ask her...

120) You've been thinking of fucking this dick all day haven't you?

121) I've been hard all day thinking about this good pussy...

Also have fun by saying ....

122) Hell yeah, work that pussy girl!

123) Yes, ride that dick girl!

124) Hell yeah bitch, just like that...

125) Take me to fuck town.

126) Harder baby!

127) Can you feel me in you?

128) I am tearing up that pussy now.

129) Fuck me baby.

130) Rub that ass all over my big cock.

131) I am gonna stuff my cock into your wet pussy.

132) Are you ready for me?

133) Tell me what you like.

The freakier she is will determine if you use "bitch", "slut", "Ho" or whatever, so I want to say here to know what she likes if you take it there. The right dirty word at the right time during sex can make her cum really hard, but you have to be sure to say it at the right time. You need to be sure that she is into being called it, because you don't want to spoil the moment. But, nine times out of ten, if you are at this level then you more than likely have nothing to worry about, and she likes being called those names and more during sex.

134) You are gonna make me fill that pussy up...

135) Oh my God you are gonna make me explode in your pussy...

136) You want to feel it deep inside?

137) You want me to make it rain?

138) I am gonna fill you up good.

139) Let me cum all over you.

140) I wanna cum in you.

141) Taste this cum.

142) You got me about to blow

All of these are good ones for when you are about to cum.

To get her cumming you could say..

143)   I want you to splash all over this dick...

144)   Gimmie that cream, baby...

145)   Cum all over my tongue...

if you are going down on her. Okay, as you can see it is beginning to get really filthy, so let's move on to the last level which is entitled just that.

The Filthy Level

When performing dirty talk (and I use the word "performing" because talking dirty may be out of your original character) the Filthy Level is about as nasty and raunchy as a person can get. There is really no limit to what you can say, and at this point she is enjoying every minute of your words. She is probably going to try to come back with words of her own, and anyone walking past your room is going to catch an earful. That being said, make sure your kids are asleep or away from the house before stepping up your dirty talk to this level, please!

146)   You like how I ram that pussy bitch?

147)   Say you love this dick...

148)   You like daddy's dick don't you?

149)   You like my big cock in you?

150)   Say you want me to cum.

151)   Tell me when you are close to cumming.

152)   You like when I take you from behind.

153)   Baby scream for me.

154)   Oh you have me cumming like a waterfall you little whore.

Also, make sure you say these lines at a nice calm vocal level. These words are strong, and there is no need to scream them, unless of course you can't help it in the moment.

155)   You like that don't you, you freaky little slut...

156)   You like the way that dick feels in your mouth/pussy, don't you?

157)   Say that's my pussy, say that's daddy's pussy...

158)   Tell me how much you like that baby.

159)   You like that dick in your ass, don't you?

160)   I am gonna pound that ass, till I explode.

161)   You like it when I slap your ass, don't you?

162)   I am gonna slam it in there.

While you are in the middle of sex and she is wailing, you will want her to say some things too. So tell her to say it!

163)   Tell me to fuck you harder baby...

164)   Tell me to beat that pussy up.

165)   Say fuck me daddy.

166)   Call me daddy.

167)   Tell me to rip that pussy.

168)   Tell me you want me to make you scream.

169)   Are you gonna swallow for me bitch?

170) Tell me you want me to hurt you.

171) Say my name bitch.

If she is usually quiet in bed, she won't be for long after your specific instructions. You will likely only have to tell her once or twice what you like to hear. After she gets it down she'll become more creative after a few times.

This one has worked wonders. First, tell her to tell you that she hates you. She might say *"What?"* Respond with *"Say it, say I hate you..."* She is going to be at a loss for words, but that's when you hit the pussy really, really hard. Go as deep as and fast as you can! Then ask her again to say it. 172) Tell me you hate me! She'll say *"I hate you!"* Then start back fucking her really hard while saying 173) Okay then, FUCK ME LIKE YOU HATE ME! She is gonna go crazy, dude.

Here are some more fun examples.

172)   Just lay back and let me stroke that pussy, baby.

173)   I love feeling your tits/ass in my hands...

174)   I love the way you taste...

Also, you can use when you climax...

175)   I'm gonna cum on your sexy ass...

176)   Shake those tits and make daddy cum on them.

177)   Daddy is about to cum on those nice lips...

178)   You want it on your tongue, here it cums...

179)   Here is some milk for those nice titties...

180)   I'm gonna cum on that pretty face...

181)   Stick out your tongue so I can drip cum on it.

182)   Feel this warm cum shoot into your pussy...

183)   Let me lick your clit till you cum baby.

184)   Tell daddy you like his nice long dick in your tight pussy.

185)   Let me see you covered in my cum.

186)   Just relax and watch me rip you apart.

187)   I'm gonna fuck you so hard, you won't be able to walk tomorrow.

188)   Shut your mouth and let me fuck it.

189)   Oh honey you got me all hard.

190)   I am gonna fuck your tight little pussy bitch!

191)   I am gonna make you scream, you little cunt.

192)   I am gonna make you speechless.

193)   Ohhh fuck you bitch, here I cum.

194)   Who is my little whore? You are.

195)   Now take this dick.

196)   I want you to beg for it.

197)   I am gonna fuck you mommy.

198)   Turn around so I can shove it up your tight little ass.

199)   Let me see those tits!

200) Harder, harder, harder, ..

Have fun.

Conclusion

Thank you again for downloading this book!

I hope this book was able to help you get good at your Dirty Talk.

The next step is to take what you've just learned and apply it to your life.

Finally, if you enjoyed this book, please take the time to share your thoughts and post a review on Amazon. It'd be greatly appreciated!

Thank you and good luck!

BDSM Positions:

The Beginner's Guide to BDSM

Check Out My Other Books!

Thanks for downloading my book! I am a firm believer that in order to have a fulfilling family life-one must be properly prepared and understand the fundamentals of relationships, how to be a good parent, and live an exciting and adventurous sex life. As you can see, I have written a series of multiple books on marriage, sex, and parenting. If you are looking to learn more about how to improve your marriage, sex and dating life, family life, etc.-please check out my other books! Simply click on the links below or search the titles below to check them out.

Parenting:

Parenting 101: 20 strategies to follow to raise well-behaved children

Raising Your Kids: Time Management for Parents for Stress-Free Parenting

Sex (General):

Sex Positions: Your Guide to the 50 Best Sex Positions for a sexy marriage!

Tantra Sex: The Beginner's Guide to 25 Tantra Techniques

Tantric Massage: Your Guide to the Best 30 Tantric Massage Techniques

BDSM Positions: The Beginner's Guide to 30 BDSM Techniques

Sex: Spice Up Your Sex Life! How to be maintain an awesome sex life with your partner and live your wildest sexual fantasies!

Sex Games: 35 Naughty Sex Games to make your Sex Life Hot!

Sex For Women:

Sexting: Sexting Tips for Women: 100 tips to turn him on!

Sex Positions for Women: The Ultimate Guide to the 50 Best Techniques to Turn Your Man On!

Talk Dirty: How to talk to get your man aroused and in the mood for sex!

Sex: The Hottest Tips for Better Orgasms!

Sex for Men:

Sex Positions for Men: The Ultimate Guide to the 50 Best Techniques to Turn Her On!

Dirty Talk: Talking Dirty for Men: 200 Examples to Get Your Girl Aroused and in the Mood for Sex!

Sex: Make her beg for more and be the best she's ever been with in bed!

Marriage:

Marriage and Sex: Why sex matters to keep romance alive!

Marriage for Women: Your Guide to a Happy, Fulfilling, Intimate Marriage!

Marriage for Men: How to be a good husband and have a happy, fulfilling, intimate marriage!

Marriage 101: How to have a long-lasting, happy and intimate marriage!

Wedding Planning: The Ultimate Guide to Budgeting and Planning your Wedding!

Marriage Communication: Your Guide to constructive praise, criticism, and communication for a happy, long-lasting marriage!

Divorce: Ten Steps to Preventing a Divorce and Save Your Marriage

Dating:

Tinder Dating: Your Guide to Creating a Strong Tinder Profile, Getting a First Date, and Being Confident!

Introduction

I want to thank you and congratulate you for downloading the book, *BDSM Positions: The Beginner's Guide to BDSM.* Downloading this book is the first step to exploring a facet of human sexuality that statistically speaking you and your partner will both enjoy at least to a mild degree. BDSM is a complex and potentially dangerous milieu of intersecting practices and kinks but it never has to evolve beyond what you and your partner are comfortable with.

This book contains proven steps and strategies on how to take BDSM experimentation one step at a time, with an emphasis on never doing more than what you and your partner are safe and comfortable exploring. The basics of BDSM can be extremely stimulating and fulfilling for most partners without ever stepping outside the bounds of mild restriction and sensation play.

Cautiously explore the following chapters and see what within piques your interest or seems as though it may pique your partner's. Remember, there is nothing wrong with a little experimentation and you won't know what you both will like until you try.

Thanks again for downloading this book, I hope you enjoy it!

Chapter 1: Defining the Rules

When the phrase BDSM comes up in conversation, many people immediately think of the extreme, leather, chains, ball gags and more than likely, plenty of pain. Unfortunately for those who never have the opportunity to experience it first hand, BDSM has come to by synonymous with only the most extreme practices which fall under the moniker when in reality BDSM encompasses a wide array of activities which run the gamut from pleasurable to painful.

For starters, lets define BDSM to allow for a better understanding of what is involved. BDSM stands for bondage, dominance, sadism and masochism. When taken as a whole BDSM can be broadly described as being dominated, restrained or otherwise made to submit to the whims of your partner. While some people take it to the next level by experiencing pleasure while either giving or receiving pain, you can have a full and adventurous time in the world of BDSM without experiencing either. As it should be with any type of sexual experience, the experiences you have dabbling with BDSM are completely and totally within your control at all times, it should never be about experiencing pleasure at the expense of your partner.

Establish Ground Rules
When first beginning to experience with BDSM it is important that you and you partner discuss in detail what is and what is not acceptable. A good first step would to be to each write out a list of things that are and are not acceptable in any sexual situation. It is important that this not be done in the heat of the moment as that can lead to a situation where a partner feels pressured into doing something that they otherwise might not be comfortable with.

When deciding on what is and is not acceptable, you should at least consider the following list of options and know how you partner feels about them.
- **How do you feel about being tied up?** This is perhaps the most basic tenant of BDSM as the loss of control can be considered an aphrodisiac to many people. Do you prefer to just have your legs or arms tied but not both? Let your partner know. If you have never been restrained

before perhaps it is best to simulate the scenario before starting for real.

- **What do you like to have done to you while you are restrained?** The degree of sexual stimulation a person enjoys while being restrained varies from person to person, some people only like to be restrained during foreplay while others prefer to be restrained during intercourse, either is fine, as is neither, as long as you and your partner are both happy.
- **What sensations do you enjoy the most?** Another core tenant of BDSM is an oscillation of sensations applied, generally while one of the partners is restrained. As such it is important to know what sensations your partner enjoys but also which they do not. Nothing ruins the mood faster than the application of stimulation that you absolutely hate.
- **Anything else that makes you uncomfortable.** If there are situations that could occur while experimenting with BDSM that you feel are absolutely off limits such as your partner leaving the room while you are bound for example should be explicitly stated beforehand. Proper planning is key to all partners having a good time.

Play safe

When experimenting with the BDSM community there are two important safety acronyms to keep in mind. RACK (risk aware consensual kink) and SSC (safe, sane, consensual). Taken together they mean that any activity you engage in should always be consensual, risky activities should never be attempted while any partner is not of sound mind and that safety should always be a number one priority.

To ensure that safety remains a top priority in any form of BDSM play it is important to have a mutually agreed upon safe word which can be used to put a stop to whatever is going on at any time. This word should be something that would not normally come up during the act such as banana or purple octopus. While this can seem like a lot of effort to put into sex without actually having any sex, the foundation of a successful BDSM relationship is a firm set of ground rules and the mutual trust to always follow them.

Start out slow
Studies show that far more people experiment with some aspect of BDSM than people think. In fact, close to 70 percent of the population can be said to have explored the idea in some detail in their sexual lifetimes. Consider this, pinning your partner's arms, spanking or blindfolding can all be considered a form of bondage. The reason that some people find the lack of control so arousing is that they find it stimulates their other senses when one is impaired.

The first thing to consider when deciding to be restrained is how you and your partner are comfortable being dressed. If your partner is intrigue by the idea of BDSM but scared at the practice, getting them used to the idea by restraining them while clothed can be a good place to start.

Blindfolding your partner will cause them to experience every sound more vividly and to use their imagination to discover what you will do to them. Likewise, restraining your partner will heighten all sense of touch. Starting off with restraints that close with Velcro is a great idea as it will give your partner the sensation of being restrained without forcing them to give up all forms of control at once. This can lead to handcuffs or even door jam or hog-tie restraints but as always it is about only doing what the other person is comfortable with.

For those who prefer to work up to even Velcro restraints, a dog collar and leash can be a good place to start. This will allow both partners to get comfortable with the idea of restricted movement without actually doing that much to restrict their movement. If you are working up to being restrained to a bed, try a dog collar, leash and a set of Velcro handcuffs.

By combining a blindfold with some form of restraints any other sensory input will be heightened to the extreme. In these situations, the subconscious tries to convince the conscious mind that the situation it finds itself in is dangerous which stimulates the senses even more. Proceed to this level cautiously however as the experience can easily overwhelm novice partners.

Chapter 2: Start with a Feather

Once all of the specifics have been discussed beforehand, the best way to begin an introductory BDSM experience is to begin by using a feather. For the remainder of this book the person who is being restrained will be referred to as the **submissive** while the other partner will be referred as the **dominant.** What many people find so enjoyable about the BDSM experience is that those in the role of submissive have no control over the sexual pleasure they are receiving while dominant partners enjoy being the gatekeeper of their partner's pleasure.

This in turn allows the dominant to experiment with numerous erotic sensations from heat, to ice, to feathers, fabrics, fingers and toys. Starting with feathers or silk is a good way to ease your partner into a BDSM experience. They excite, tickle and arouse the skin with just the simplest touch. Start by restraining your partner lightly and running the soft item around their erogenous zones, experiment and see what you both enjoy the most. As previously discussed, BDSM experiences do not need to include situations when the dominant violates the submissive while they are restrained. Finding the right mix of stimuli to bring your partner to the absolute heights of pleasure should be a fun sexual adventure for you both.

Try your tongue
While your partner is restrained, try experimenting with the pleasure you can provide with just your tongue alone. Experiment with your partner's neck, mouth, face, chest and other erogenous zones. If the submissive is both restrained and blindfolded the variety of sensations available from a combination of sucking, licking and kissing will drive your partner wild. Tease with quick flicks of the tongue, blow gently on their most sensitive areas or lightly bite them with your

teeth. Oral sex as part of the BDSM experience can be completely different experience than when done in a non-BDSM situations. The dominant will completely control the experience as the submissive is helpless to influence their own orgasm. Those looking to enhance the experience further can look into a variety of products including warming gels, ice or even Altoids.

Move on to toys
Contrary to popular conceptions, dominants take pleasure in providing pleasure to their partners, the fact that this pleasure can be derived from pain is irrelevant. After you and your partner have experimented with the pleasure derived from using your mouth and soft things such as silk scarves or feathers, you might be ready to try something a little more intense. When a submissive is both restrained and blindfolded the noise that many sex toys make can be as stimulating as the pleasure it provides. Starting with a simple vibrator will allow the dominant to tease all of their partner's erogenous zones whether that partner is male or female. Adding warming gels or massage oils in tandem can increase your partner's sensations even further.

Depending on what you and your partner have discussed prior to beginning to experiment in the realm of BDSM teasing with sex toys can be extended to full on penetration. Remember, do not take this step without first discussing it with your partner as some people do not like to be penetrated while restrained. With the level of consent determined it is always important to have lubrication handy before moving on to insertion. The type of toy can vastly affect the type of stimulation it provides. If you and you partner are experimenting with this type of play for the first time it is best to start with several different low cost toys, see which provide the most pleasure and then go from there.

Taking it to the next level

If you and your partner have experimented with a variety of BDSM foreplay scenarios and are both comfortable taking it to the next level, then participating in consensual restrained sex is the next erotic step. Moving on to penetrative sex with restraints allows the dominant to be in full control of the coitus while the submissive once more is solely at their whim to as to the pleasure provided.

If you and your partner are interested in taking things up a notch in another way, it may be time to experiment to determine if a little bit of pain can lead to a whole lot more pleasure. Spanking and biting cause excess blood to flow to the affected area which then increases the stimulation felt in the affected area. Many people enjoy having their nipples pinched lightly or a restrained spanking and when experimenting in this arena this is the best place to start. The most important thing is to start off slowly and build the sensations from there and experimenting with different blends of pleasure and pain. Everyone has a different pain threshold which is why this step should be explored with extreme caution.

Suggested Items
The following items can be considered essentially for anyone investigating the BDSM experience.

Rope: Statistically speaking most people have some bit of rope lying around that could, in a pinch, be used to restrain a submissive. This is a mindset that many budding BDSM enthusiasts find themselves in but in reality, the type of rope matters. Most rope is to rough or hard to restrain a person without rubbing the skin raw, especially if you plan on having penetrative sex while restrained. Using the wrong rope can end a BDSM experience before it fully begins so do yourself a favor and purchase bondage rope, it will be designed not leave marks, be machine washable and most importantly be nice and soft when it comes in contact with skin. Nylon rope available at most hardware stores is generally considered the next best thing.

Handcuffs: Another BDSM staple, handcuffs provide less readily available variety than rope and should be considered if your partner does not like their legs to be restrained. These days, handcuffs come in three major varieties.

- *Traditional metal handcuffs* are cheap, easy to use and as a bonus can easily add a bit of roleplay to the proceedings. The biggest downside to these cuffs is their lack of padding, which may or may not be an issue depending on the submissive's pain tolerance. Non-official versions also tend to break easily.
- *Padded handcuffs:* When first starting out experimenting with BDSM scenarios these are most likely the cuffs you will want to try first. They are much thicker than traditional cuffs so they will not leave marks and they are generally sealed using Velcro so a new submissive won't have anything to worry about. They tend to be more expensive than metal cuffs, though not by much. When looking for padded cuffs be sure to look online at customer reviews to ensure that what you pick will be up to the challenge.
- *Bondage Tape:* While not a pair of handcuffs per se, bondage tape is a relatively new product which promises to only stick to itself and not your hair or your skin. It is as easy to remove as it is to put on and, even better, its reusable. This product is cheap, inconspicuous and can be used for more than just cuffs. For beginning BDSM enthusiasts this is most likely the best bet.

Blindfold

While it may seem that there are many items which can be used in place of a blindfold, few do the job as well as an item designed for the task. A quality blindfold will prevent all light from getting through, while still remaining comfortable for the submissive and easy to put on and remove. Dealing with a substitute can be difficult as well as time consuming and can easily ruin the mood. Do yourself a favor and pick up a proper blindfold, you can generally find them sold as sleep masks at most pharmacies for around $20.

Household Items

When beginning your BDSM adventure there are several common household items that can be used to enhance the experience so you and your partner can determine what you enjoy without putting a lot of money down of items you may or may not use.

- *Pastry brush:* A common pastry brush can be used in place of a feather to provide an introduction to what is broadly referred to as "sensation play"
- *Spatula:* If you or your partner are interested in investigating your feelings on spanking further then a spatula will be your best bet. Silicone spatulas work best for beginners. Wooden or metal spatulas should be worked up to. Remember, never use silicone based lube on any silicone items as it will ruin them.
- *Snake Bite Kit:* While seemingly both innocuous and incredibly un-sexy most snake bites kits tend to come with a pair of suction cups that are ideal when experimenting with nipple play before moving on to more robust options such as clips or clamps.

Chapter 3: Starter Positions

After you and your partner have experimented with the basic aspects of BDSM the following list and description of various bondage positions can help you take the experience to the next level. As with everything else concerning BDSM it is important to discuss what you and your partner are comfortable with before proceeding.

Ball Tie: The Ball Tie is a position in which the goal is to place the submissive into a position resembling a ball. The legs should be secured in such a way that the thighs press against the chest. The hands can be restrained either in front of or behind the back. The position can be considered both stringent and stimulating while still remaining comfortable.

Breast Bondage: This technique involves tying a woman in such a way that they accentuate the breasts, and is more about the look than any restrictive effect. This form of restraint can be performed with clothes or without. The most basic form involves placing a rope around the torso slightly above the breasts then adding a second rope tied just bellowed them. Finally, a third roped is then looped over the shoulders to lie between the breasts so it can be drawn over the other ropes to hold them tightly together.

Crotch Rope: This technique ties a rope around a woman's waist in such a way that the rope passes between the labia for the purpose of applying stimulating pleasure to the region. Specific forms of this technique can be adapted to apply to men as well. In general, the rope slips between the labia majora or past the vulva cleft. Depending on the fashion in which the knots are tied it can also apply pressure to the clitoris or anus depending. The rope is typically attached above the hips and draped across the genitals before being tied off and slipped down and around to connect back to its source on the other side.

Frog Tie: This technique binds a person's legs in such a way that their legs are held so that the feet are near the inner-thighs. Each ankle is restrained to its adjacent thigh and the arms are then placed behind the back as each arm is connected to the thigh as well. This position allows for a vulnerable but not completely immobile restraint. For a more advanced form of this technique bind the submissive's wrists to their opposite ankles for a more stringent restraint.

Head Bondage: This type of bondage technique can be broken down into two categories. The first involves the use of a bondage hood, which may include a blindfold as well as a gag as well as a heavy collar or other attachment points for more involved BDSM experiences. It may also refer to the use of rope or a similar item to restrict head movement. A head harness, perhaps more so than other techniques discussed previously creates more of a sense of objectification and helplessness in the submissive and should be first performed in a situation where the submissive can be easily removed if needed.

Hog Tie: This technique involves binding the submissive's wrists and ankles before fastening both sets of extremities behind the back while they are lying face down. The legs are then bent at the knees and connected to a restraint which run the length of the body, holding them up in the air. When attempting this position, it is important to know that it places a large amount of pressure on the abdomen which in turn can make it difficult for the submissive to breathe. As such it is very important to ensure that the submissive can breathe freely at all stages of this form of restraint.

Spread Eagle Tie: This technique involves restraining the submissive in such a way that they are readily in a position to encourage sexual stimulation. This technique involves securing the submissive to three or four separate points depending on if an X or Y spread eagle is desired. This position is popularly used with a Saint Andrews Cross but a sturdy bedframe will work just as well. For a Y spread eagle simple connect the submissive's hands together above their head instead of separately. A spread eagle can be performed with either the submissive face up or face down although the face down method inherently produces risks of asphyxiation.

Over-arm Tie: The over-arm technique is a positon whereby the submissive's arms are restrained behind their head by ropes or other types of restraints which are connected to their ankles. The over-arm tie is another form of tie that is often used as much for the aesthetic affect as it is to restrict movement and as such it is often combined with additional bondage techniques including the crotch rope or a modified version of the frog tie. If you and your partner are looking for something a little more restrictive it can easily be combined with the hog tie or the shrimp tie.

Reverse Prayer: This technique requires a the submissive's arms to be bound behind them in the opposite position they would be in if they folded their arms in prayer. To enact this position, the submissive must place their hands between their shoulders while keeping the fingers of both hands extended and their palms touching. The wrists are then bound together with a series of restrains before a rope is looped around the chest and drawn over the wrists to hold them in place. This technique is uncomfortable for many people and can lead to cramps over time. When attempting this position, it is important not to overdo it so that the submissive's elbows are touching as this can easily lead to dislocation.

Rope Harness: This technique involves binding the submissive in a complex web of restraints to hold them up completely. This technique requires between 30 and 45 feet of rope to try and will require much practice to do correctly. Start by tying a bowline knot around one leg. Take the long end of the rope and tie another bowline knot around the other leg. Wrap the remaining length of rope around the back and through the crotch area to form a diamond shape. Continue following the same basic pattern as you move up the body. This technique can be more or less restrictive depending on if you wrap the arms or wrap the rope under the arms.

Shrimp Tie: This technique first gained popularity in Japan more than 300 years ago as a means of interrogation and torture, as such, which this form of bondage can be great in short doses, a prolonged session can cause intense discomfort. To begin, the submissive sits with their legs crossed and their hands behind their back. Begin by binding the ankles together before connecting that restraint to one that is looped around the submissive's neck (with plenty of breathing room) which is then attached to the ankles. The arms are then bound behind the back and that restraint is also connected to the main restraint.

Suspension bondage: As the name implies, this technique involves hanging the submissive from a single or several overhead suspension points. The type of suspension can be either horizontal or vertical, partial or complete, but always carries a higher level of risk than the techniques discussed above. The main goal in suspension activities is to create an even greater sense of restraint and vulnerability in the submissive as the act of trying to free themselves becomes more inherently dangerous. Vertical suspension is generally achieved by lifting the submissive from the ground by their wrists, horizontal suspension is generally achieved by utilizing a hog tie position and inverted suspension in achieved by lifting the submissive from the ground using their legs. These positions can easily restrict the submissive's airway if not done properly and extreme caution should always be used for the submissive's safety.

Strappado Bondage: This term is used to describe a technique in which the submissive's arms are bound behind their back then attached to a suspension point above. The submissive's legs can either be secured to one another or to another point on the ground. The submissive's arms are then elevated in such a way that they are required to bend forward. The term strappado comes from a form of torture still used in some countries to this day. This form of bondage must be practiced carefully as it can easily cause permanent damage to the submissive's arms and shoulder's if jerked to forcefully.

Japanese bondage: Called Kinbaku which means "the beauty of tight binding" this technique involves binding the submissive's buttocks in an erotically attractive pattern. This type of bondage can include binding the wrists either together or separate, binding the hands either in front of or behind the back, using a diamond pattern and binding while either standing or suspended. Many of the techniques in Kinbaku can be complicated and thus open to a higher degree of risk and should only be explored further when both you and your partner feel the need for advanced techniques.

Classic Damsel: So named for the way the submissive lays, the elbows are tied together so they are touching behind the back, the wrists are connected together and the legs are restrained together below the knees as well as the ankles.

Legs Up Ball Tie: This is a variation on the classic ball tie. You start by binding the submissive's waste and thighs together, you then bind the arms to the ankles so both are straight out. One or both sets of restraints will need to be attached to a secure point above her head.

Tiptoe crotch rope spreader bar strappado: In this position the ankles are connected to a spreader bar. The submissive is then asked to stand on tiptoe while their elbows are bound together behind the back. The crotch rope is primarily used as decoration and additional stimulation.

Yoke Positon: This position simulates the barnyard implement of the same name and requires a sturdy pole as well as rope. When attaching a pole at neck height be very careful to not restrict the breathing. Place the pole on the back of the neck and secure the arms to it before securing the neck.

Crab Position: In this position the submissive sits with their back bent forward so their hands reach their feet. The arms are then bound to the legs at the wrist and again at the elbow. The submissive then leans back and balances on their buttocks.

Chair Position: This position is perfect for restraining a submissive over a piece of furniture. Have the submissive bend over the chair and restrain them the way you would with a ball tie. Then bind them to the chair above the elbow and above the knee. The hands and feet can also be bound.

Waitress Position: The term "waitress" refers to any position where the hands are restrained in front of the body while the elbows are restrained behind. The severity of the position desired determines at what point the elbows are bound though right above the elbow is considered standard.

Double V: In this position the submissive's arms are restrained together with each hand gripping the opposite shoulder. The hands are tied to the upper arm and bound together at the elbow as well. The submissive sits with their legs folded and a rope binds the feet and attaches to the arms.

The Offering: In this position the submissive's hands are bound together overhead while the legs are held apart either side to side or in a lunging pose. Remember when the arms are bound above the head always ensure that the submissive can breathe easily. Use caution.

Caterpillar: Any position that involves wrapping the submissive completely in rope can be referred to as a caterpillar. Similar to a rope web though more elaborate it can be considered mainly decorative though due to its nature it does make an effective leg binding option. Typically, the rope runs the length of the body while the hands are restrained above the head.

Bottoms Up: In this position the submissive is placed in a crotch rope which is attached to a point overhead. The submissive kneels on their hands and knees and their feet and hands are then bound together.

Olympic Mascot: In this position the submissive is made to bend over and touch their toes. They are then fitted with a crotch rope attached to a point overhead. Their feet and hands are each bound separately before finally being connected with together by a short length of rope.

Box Tie Position: This position is used in many more elaborate positions as well. In it the submissive places their arms behind their back so each hand is grabbing the opposite arm above the elbow. The wrists are then bound together and connected to a restraint which wraps around the front of the body both above and below the breasts.

Hooplah: In this position the submissive first places their arms behind their back the arms are then bound by wrapping them repeatedly from wrist to above the shoulder. A second restraint is then looped around the submissive's neck and above and below the wrists before connecting around the back to the wrists.

The Stardust: In this position the submissive places their hands behind their back so that one hand lays on each buttocks. Restraints are then wrapped around the body including the hands at the hips, and the stomach and those two are connected together. Then again above and below the wrists which are then also connected together. The two sections are then connected together.

Diving Springboard: In this position the submissive starts on the ground with their legs sticking up in the air. The legs are bound together between the knee and the calf before binding the ankles together. The wrists are then bound together and connected to the ankles. The ankles are then connected to a point above the head.

Conclusion

Thank you again for downloading this book! I hope it was able to help you to begin to explore the complex and erotic world of BDSM experimentation. Remember, when first starting out it is important to discuss the specifics in detail with your partner and to always perform BDSM practices responsibly by considering RACK and SCC before committing to anything. Finally, always be aware of which types of activities need to be practiced with extra caution, nothing will ruin the mood faster than having to call 911 because your partner nearly asphyxiated because you hog-tied them improperly.

The next step is to put down this book already and find a partner you feel comfortable discussing the erotic possibilities that BDSM can provide, your more fulfilling sex life will thank you.

Finally, if you enjoyed this book, then I'd like to ask you for a favor, would you be kind enough to leave a review for this book on Amazon? It'd be greatly appreciated!

Made in the USA
Las Vegas, NV
27 December 2024

15481396R00105